A NEIGHBORHOOD POLITICS OF LAST RESORT

MCGILL-QUEEN'S STUDIES IN URBAN GOVERNANCE
Series editors: Kristin Good and Martin Horak

In recent years there has been an explosion of interest in local politics and the governance of cities – both in Canada and around the world. Globally, the city has become a consequential site where instances of social conflict and of cooperation play out. Urban centres are increasingly understood as vital engines of innovation and prosperity and a growing body of interdisciplinary research on urban issues suggests that high-performing cities have become crucial to the success of nations, even in the global era. Yet at the same time, local and regional governments continue to struggle for political recognition and for the policy resources needed to manage cities, to effectively govern, and to achieve sustainable growth.

The purpose of the McGill-Queen's Studies in Urban Governance series is to highlight the growing importance of municipal issues, local governance, and the need for policy reform in urban spaces. The series aims to answer the question "why do cities matter?" while exploring relationships between levels of government and examining the changing dynamics of metropolitan and community development. By taking a four-pronged approach to the study of urban governance, the series encourages debate and discussion of: (1) actors, institutions, and how cities are governed; (2) policy issues and policy reform; (3) the city as case study; and (4) urban politics and policy through a comparative framework.

With a strong focus on governance, policy, and the role of the city, this series welcomes manuscripts from a broad range of disciplines and viewpoints.

A NEIGHBORHOOD POLITICS OF LAST RESORT

Post-Katrina New Orleans and the Right to the City

STEPHEN DANLEY

McGill-Queen's University Press

Montreal & Kingston · London · Chicago

© McGill-Queen's University Press 2018

ISBN 978-0-7735-5488-7 (cloth)
ISBN 978-0-7735-5489-4 (paper)
ISBN 978-0-7735-5589-1 (ePDF)
ISBN 978-0-7735-5590-7 (ePUB)

Legal deposit fourth quarter 2018
Bibliothèque nationale du Québec

Printed in Canada on acid-free paper that is 100% ancient forest free
(100% post-consumer recycled), processed chlorine free

This book has been published with the help of a grant from Rutgers University
Research Council.

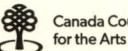

| Funded by the Government of Canada | Financé par le gouvernement du Canada | Canada | | Canada Council for the Arts | Conseil des arts du Canada |

We acknowledge the support of the Canada Council for the Arts, which
last year invested $153 million to bring the arts to Canadians throughout
the country.

Nous remercions le Conseil des arts du Canada de son soutien. L'an dernier,
le Conseil a investi 153 millions de dollars pour mettre de l'art dans la vie
des Canadiennes et des Canadiens de tout le pays.

Library and Archives Canada Cataloguing in Publication

Danley, Stephen D., author
    A neighborhood politics of last resort:
    post-Katrina New Orleans and the right to the city / Stephen Danley.

    (McGill-Queen's studies in urban governance; 10)
    Includes bibliographical references and index.
    Issued in print and electronic formats.
    ISBN 978-0-7735-5488-7 (cloth). – ISBN 978-0-7735-5489-4 (paper). –
    ISBN 978-0-7735-5589-1 (ePDF). – ISBN 978-0-7735-5590-7 (ePUB)

    1. Neighborhoods – Political aspects – Louisiana – New Orleans – Case studies.
    2. Social advocacy – Louisiana – New Orleans – Case studies. 3. Social
    movements – Louisiana – New Orleans – Case studies. 4. Citizens' associations –
    Louisiana – New Orleans – Case studies. 5. Community life – Louisiana –
    New Orleans – Case studies. 6. Hurricane Katrina, 2005 – Social aspects –
    Louisiana – New Orleans – Case studies. 7. New Orleans (La.) – Social
    conditions – 21st century – Case studies. 8. Case studies – I. Title. II. Series:
    McGill-Queen's studies in urban governance; 10

HN80.N45D36 2018   307.3'362160976335   C2018-903585-4
                                                       C2018-903586-2

This book was typeset by Marquis Interscript in 10.5/13 Sabon.

Contents

Tables and Figures

Acknowledgments

In New Orleans, everyone has a hustle. This is your hustle.

Karen Gadbois

Monologist Spalding Gray referred to his first book as a "monster in a box." Like the slaying of any monster, completing this book required a wide cast of heroes.

To those who worked with me academically, including supervisor Robert Walker, mentor John DiIulio, and professor Teresa Smith,

To those in New Orleans who taught me to love New Orleans, particularly Karen Gadbois and Mama Jennifer (Jennifer Turner),

To the local leaders who welcomed me to their neighborhoods and gave of their time,

To the friends and family who provided feedback, suggested readings, and kept me sane, especially my lovely wife Sue Altman, mother and father Teresa and Douglas Danley, siblings Kristen and John Danley, unofficial editor Cynthia Ludvigsen, fellow Marshall Scholar Stephen Silvius, high school classmate Brian Murphy, and New Orleans friend Meg Lousteau,

To the *Journal of Cosmopolitan Civil Society* for seeing something in this research and publishing an article based on the findings that later evolved to Chapter 6,

And to the Marshall Commission, the Robert A. Fox Leadership Program at the University of Pennsylvania and the Rutgers Research Council for their generous financial support.

Thank you from the bottom of my heart.

A NEIGHBORHOOD POLITICS OF LAST RESORT

The Cult of Community

Community has become a cult, an object of warm-and-fuzzy ritual worship for politicians of all stripes, academics and the rapidly expanding new class of social commentators. Nobody can get enough of the c-word.

Gibson and Cameron (2001)

Early writing on urban governance and community elites largely leaves community out of the picture (Abzug 2008). For example, in Dahl's (1961) famous treatise on urban governance, set in New Haven, communities are largely absent from the wider discussion of who has power. Dahl highlights political elites as the center of urban politics. Hunter (1969), in a study of what is now known to be Atlanta, looks past communities to highlight the power of economic elites in urban communities. For these authors, communities appear solely on the fringes, subjugated to the influence of powerful local elites. More recently, however, community has made a comeback. Gibson and Cameron (2001) argue that community is fashionable for academics, politicians, and activists. Activists claim *the real power is with the community*, scholars claim *the real knowledge is with the community* (Chaskin and Garg 1997), and politicians listen intently to community with great results.

This book is about neither of these narratives – it is neither a reaffirmation that elites hold power over communities (though they sometimes do) nor a celebration of community influence (though communities sometimes deserve celebration). It is about the messy ways in which urban neighborhoods – communities of place (Smith 1999) – advocate for their communities. It is about the good that neighborhood associations can do, but also about their dark underbelly. It is about discrimination. It is about "not-in-my-backyardism"

(NIMBYism) that looks at a renter or a person of color and says *I don't want them to live here*. It is about New Orleans, and about how in the aftermath of Hurricane Katrina, quirky neighborhood organizations found an unlikely moment in the limelight, both for good and for ill.

In New Orleans, these neighborhood associations were the sites of neighbors seeking to reconnect after the storm and of fierce advocacy for neighborhood issues. They pushed back against undemocratic policy and demonstrated discrimination and ugliness. That dichotomy – that communities can be such an important democratic force while also being messy, problematic, and, at times, discriminatory – is the heart of this book. It is a book about democracy and justice, and how the two intertwine with place and race.

After Hurricane Katrina, New Orleans became the heart of a pushback against a technocratic approach to public policy. Policy experts inundated the city (recruited in part by then Lt Governor Mitch Landreui, who would later become mayor), eager to try the newest, most modern, and highest-impact policy ideas. Planners attempted to remake the city to eliminate residential housing and even commercial development in areas more likely to flood. Health care clinics proliferated through the city in an attempt to bring health care closer to residents' lives. The school system was reimagined without boundaries, so that any child could attend any of the multitude of charter schools cropping up throughout the city. And New Orleanians protested all of it. They protested not just the policy changes, but the way they were enacted and the exclusion of residents in the planning and development of policy changes. A fierce localism became central to city politics. Local activists took a defiant stance towards changes. Ashley Morris, a local professor who became an overnight blogging sensation, created a rallying cry of *Fuck You You Fucking Fucks* in response to rumors that the beloved Saints might move to San Antonio. Though Morris passed away in the years following the storm, his defiant attitude towards those remaking the city was memorialized both in David Simon's television show *Tremé* and annually in the local "Rising Tide" conference where the city's most influential blogger receives a prize named after Morris. Search protests and you can still find *FYYFF* shirts memorializing Morris's most famous blog post. The same attitude was sarcastically captured by Roberta Gratz (2015) in her aptly named book *We're Still Here Ya Bastards*. Gratz writes:

The elitist vision for New Orleans's future was quite a Christmas present for those still suffering in the aftermath of the storms. It was a sure indicator of what was to come from the most prestigious and powerful people of the city, for whom it is difficult to grasp that what is seemingly logical might not be right for the city. Planning rhetoric always appears so logical at first glance.

As we will see in Chapter 1, neighborhood associations improbably became a public counterbalance to experts inundating the city with policy ideas. At the core of that resistance was the idea that *community* should make community decisions.

Unlike the efforts of the Christian Right in the United States, this movement does not focus primarily on finding, nominating, and supporting candidates for elected office (see Rozell and Wilcox 1995). It intersects with other social movements (Piven and Cloward 1979), community organizing (Alinsky 1971), and particularly with what Lefebvre (1943, 158) famously calls "the Right to the City" and Purcell (2002, 100) calls a "politics of inhabitants." In New Orleans, similar language was adopted by advocates of public housing who argued that New Orleanians had a "right to return" (Johnson 2011a, 192). The common strain across these latter ideas is the manner in which the experience of those living in a city is set up as sacrosanct. The community has a right to its city and as such must be a central actor in its politics. Gratz's (2015) book is a celebration of this community pluck.

Neighborhood associations somewhat improbably became the heart of that New Orleans neighborhood movement. Leontidou (2010) writes that one element of the right to the city is control over urban space – that those who occupy such space, even if they do not own property, should have additional rights over it. Neighborhood associations are founded on a similar principle. Logan and Rabrenovic (1990, 68) theorize that "a neighborhood association is defined as a civic organization oriented toward maintaining or improving the quality of life in a geographically delimited residential area." In post-Katrina New Orleans, neighborhood associations emerged in the popular zeitgeist as not just protectors of their own turf, but as protectors of the threatened soul of the city. It was a narrative so powerful that the city's most prominent neighborhood association leader launched a political career based upon her popular neighborhood work and that she eventually became the city's first female mayor. It is no coincidence that a mayor who asked policy experts from around the world to try their ideas in the city was replaced by a mayor whose neighborhood work fought against those very same experts.

But attend a neighborhood association meeting and a different picture of the neighborhood movement emerges. There is a strange rhythm to these gatherings. Gone is the soaring rhetoric of "rights." Neighborhood associations can be stoically formal, with an almost comical adherence to Robert's Rules of Order. Votes are taken on things as mundane as accepting the previous meeting's minutes, causing attendees to fidget and wonder why they took the time to attend. That feeling is accentuated as one or two detailed-oriented neighborhood leaders derail entire meetings by speaking at length on neighborhood minutiae, often on an issue of which other residents are blissfully unaware. From the back seat of a community center gymnasium or a church pew where so many neighborhood associations have their meetings, little of the promise of the right to the city is evident. Yes, during election season that pew may be shared with a candidate for city council, or even a judge running for office, but more often the pew is empty and the meeting is spent on the mundane. The Fontainebleau Improvement Association annually pays to spray local trees for caterpillars. The Gentilly Terrace and Gardens Neighborhood Association holds a neighborhood yard sale. The Pilotland Neighborhood Association conducts "blight walks" to identify homes at risk of falling down.

These hardly seem the dramatic actions of community that promise to remake a city's politics in the image of the people's needs. Worse still, focusing on place and neighborhood has its own dark history in the United States. Purcell (2002) writes of how the South used place, culture, and history to enforce Jim Crow laws, actively discriminating against and harming African-Americans. Similarly, Delmont (2016) writes that opposition to school busing and the integration of schools depended heavily on place-based organizations that argued against busing so as to maintain the character of the neighborhood. These are extreme examples, but they are indicative of the challenges to social justice inherent in empowering local neighborhood organizations. Purcell (2002, 100) writes that the right to the city "is disconcerting because we cannot know what kind of a city these new urban politics will produce." Will it be a politics of empowerment or one of discrimination?

In this book, I ask this question of New Orleans, but also use New Orleans and its associations to address larger challenges to the cult of community. I lay out the theory and potential pitfalls of the right to the city, arguing that the New Orleans neighborhood movement embraces elements of the right to the city while rejecting others (Chapter 1). I introduce neighborhood associations and examine their potential to counterbalance "neoliberalism" (Chapter 2) – which is little – but also lay out their potential to reframe urban politics (Chapter 3) – which is more promising. I look at their role in the democratic infrastructure of the city (Chapter 4) and the manner in which the right to the city both complements and undermines democratic justice. And I examine the ways in which neighborhood associations can undermine social justice (Chapter 5) and the extreme approaches neighborhood activists use to forward their agendas (Chapter 6).

What emerges is a new story, one that rejects the old narrative of "elites" running cities and shows that local communities play critical roles in governance, but one that also rejects the new cult of community, which sees community input as a type of cure-all to be propagated by volunteers with wide smiles. Instead, I find a politics of last resort in which neighborhood activists are drawn into tedious neighborhood fights because of failures across other governmental systems, and in which democratic and social justice are fragile and easily abused. Local empowerment comes with risk, and those who take its mantle perform a service to their communities while often perpetuating existing stereotypes and risk. Democracy in neighborhoods, much as in cities, states, and nations, is applied unevenly, and the interest of some (particularly homeowners) are favored over the interests of others (particularly vulnerable populations at risk of facing discrimination or facing economic challenges). This type of neighborhood politics is a last resort, not a community cure-all.

1

The Right to New Orleans

If I have to participate one more time, I'm going to scream.
> Louise, executive director of the Vieux Carré
> Property Owners, Residents, and Associates

Frank, the president of the Algiers Point Association, said it best: "We [in neighborhood associations] don't actually have any formal power, but like most cities, if a neighborhood association shows up with a few people, the city listens."

That quote is at odds with the way the New Orleans neighborhood movement was discussed when I first began this study some three years after Hurricane Katrina. Gone is the romantic notion that participation changes a city through a neighborhood movement. It is replaced by a stranger notion: change is brought about by a few dedicated volunteers. Or, perhaps more accurately, that a few local volunteers can force a city to listen. This chapter lays out the theoretical foundation for the book – it discusses urban social movements, community organizing, and the right to the city. It discusses how these wider movements connect to the New Orleans neighborhood movement and the way that movement can and should inform other place-based movements in other cities. And most critically, it lays out the ways that a neighborhood movement intersects with, and even undermines, efforts at social and racial justice.

At the heart of that story are the efforts of the New Orleans's neighborhood movement in the years after Hurricane Katrina. This work, grounded in ethnography and the interviews that took place as the city recovered, leads with an empirical examination of that movement. It was a time when New Orleans neighborhoods took center stage, when they appeared as a bastion of local input to policy processes that felt both technocratic and globalized to returning residents. I argue that the movement is misunderstood and romanticized, that the neighborhood movement was one of last resort, able to empower communities with little influence, but at risk of entrenching racial and socio-economic divides built into New Orleans's geography and America's history. In a moment when grassroots organizing and *resistance* is gaining momentum in the United States in response to the election of President Donald Trump and when "subterranean politics" focused on restoring democracy is gaining prevalence internationally (Kaldor and Selchow 2013), the New Orleans case has resonance: it tackles the challenges (and inequities) of local organizing grounded in place. It is one answer to the question of *what comes next* after marches, protest, and resistance.

That answer comes in the context of a long history of urban social movements and community organizing. This book is both informed by that history and a contribution to it. Elements of the New Orleans neighborhood movement mirror key works on grassroots movements. As in Piven and Cloward's *Poor People's Movements* (1979), New Orleans neighborhood activists lean heavily on informal organizing, going so far as to intentionally keep organizations from gaining too much structure or becoming established political entities. As with Alinsky's (1971) *Rules for Radicals*, neighborhood leaders often picked parochial conflicts that kept out of traditional partisan politics, prioritizing local struggles specific to a community (and like Alinsky's organizing model, New Orleans neighborhood groups struggled to deal with the ways race fractured those local communities). As in Polletta's (2002) study of participatory democracy, neighborhood associations struggle to balance democratic principles with practical goals.

At the center of the New Orleans neighborhood renaissance are concepts of place and community. Place and community have long been a part of the city movement lexicon: Mayer (2009) traces the slogans of urban social movements, highlighting Europe's use of "Let's take the city!" (Lotta Continua 1972 as in Mayer 2009, 363) and the North American use of "community control" (Fainstein and Fainstein 1974 as in Mayer 2009, 363). More prominently, Mayer argues that Lefebvre's (1943) formulation of the right to the city has been adopted by both scholars and activists at the forefront of a variety of urban social movements. The history and usage of that rallying cry is complex, and its intersections with the New Orleans neighborhood movement even more so.

In 1943, Lefebvre called the *right to the city* a cry and a demand, a slogan that can both highlight difficulties and disparities in urban life and serve as a rallying cry for addressing them. The rallying cry stuck. Recently, city advocates and others have picked up this cry, using it to address a wide variety of issues, including "conflicts over housing (Grant Building Tenants Association 2001; Olds, 1998), patriarchal cities (City & Shelter et al., no date; United Nations Center for Human Settlements 2001), participatory planning (Daniel 2001), and social exclusion in cities more generally (Buroni, 1998; Cities for Human Rights, 1998; Worldwide Conference on the Right to Cities Free from Discrimination and Inequality, 2002)" (Purcell 2002, 101). Mitchell (2003) uses it to address homelessness, and Balzarini and Shlay (2016) to address development.

Attoh (2011, 678) argues that "[t]he ability to link the rights of bus riders to those of the homeless or those of welfare recipients must be seen as a strength. The right to the city is, in this sense, strategically fuzzy. That fuzziness is grounded in the phrase's lack of formal definition."

With increased usage, Lefebvre's (1943, 158) claim that the right to the city should be a "transformed and renewed right to urban life" continues to be reexamined. Marcuse (2009) addresses who should have the right to the city, centering on vulnerable communities and arguing that the right needs to be explicitly oriented towards justice. That the right to the city should be focused on the vulnerable is contested, which Harvey (2008, xv) acknowledges, arguing that "the right to the city is an empty signifier. Everything depends on who gets to fill it with meaning." Mitchell (2003) focuses on legal rights – particularly of vulnerable communities such as the homeless – to use public spaces. Attoh (2011, 676) follows in this tradition, diving into the disputes over the "type" of right contained in the right to the city and arguing that there are multiple schools that define the right in different ways: "[w]hile David Harvey among others defines the right to the city as a collective right to the democratic management of urban resources, Don Mitchell's work on homelessness speaks to the ways in which a right to the city may also be conceived of as a right against 'democratic' management."

Harvey's (2012, 136) wider and more democratic conception of the right to the city highlights the role of global markets that put neoliberal pressure on cities. He argues "why cannot the 'right to the city' become a key mobilizing slogan for anti-capitalist struggle?" That formulation of the right to the city puts the right to the city in opposition to the growing globalized financial pressures on cities that push them towards neoliberal reforms. Johnson (2011a, ix) argues that neoliberalism "is too often conflated with classic laissez-faire economics and 'smaller government.' Neoliberalization does not entail a comprehensive reduction of state spending or capacities; instead, this process crafts a regulatory regime that most enhances the conditions of capital accumulation." Put more simply, neoliberalism is "the activist promotion of a new order of market rule" (Johnson 2011a, xx–xxi) in which government is recast as "the market's handmaiden." Cities facing such pressure can succumb to a variety of policies that undermine the right of residents, including what Harvey (2012, 105) calls "Disneyfication" in which a city focuses its development policy explicitly on attracting rich residents or tourists, and in doing so turns the city into an amusement park for those with resources. Balzarini and Shlay (2016, 504) define the right to the city as explicitly about control over development, arguing in a study about casino development that the "right to the city is about power: who should rightfully have the power to make a community and who should have a say in decisions about urban development." De Souza (2001) works from the Brazilian tradition of the right to the city, using participatory budgeting as an example of community control over resources.

Purcell (2002) highlights a different component of this argument, arguing that the right to the city is fundamentally about a politics that centers, in terms of physical space, inhabitants of the city. He puts geography and, potentially, localism at the center of a new political philosophy in an attempt to move the discussion and study surrounding the right to the city beyond being a tool for advocacy and into a coherent philosophy that guides city governance. Leontidou (2010) iterates further, centering the right to the city as about specific rights to specific places furthering Mitchell's (2003) conceptions of the right to the city as an individual right stemming from the use of public space. Leontidou (2010, 1188) focuses on specific urban spaces, writing about a "shift of the balance within the 'right to the city': from the right to inhabit (as squatters) to the right to occupy and use public spaces, to gather and protest in city centres, where convergence spaces materialize (Routledge and Cumbers, 2009: pp. 89–101)." In this formulation of the right to the city, physical space is central to the concept – with a focus on claiming unused spaces.

Mayer (2009) takes these theoretical debates a step further, arguing that there is a gap between the radical vision of theorists and what is happening when activists adopt the right to the city as a slogan. Mayer

(2009, 367) argues that "the movements out there, in the real world, are invoking this claim in rather different ways." It is here that the New Orleans movement and the right to the city intersect. In New Orleans, neighborhood associations adopted elements of the right to the city – particularly the focus on the rights of those who use and live in urban spaces to have power over its development in a way that extends past their accumulated capital. Neighborhood movements gain their legitimacy from their geography; the idea that living in a neighborhood should give residents control beyond their own property line is parallel to (if distinct from) Lefebvre's (1943) conception of a right to the city and the legitimacy that comes from living in the city. Critiques and challenges of the right to the city are similarly parallel to critiques and challenges of a politics grounded in neighborhood movements.

Many of the challenges identified by scholars within the right to the city manifested themselves during the New Orleans neighborhood movement: is the right to the city a democratic boon to the vulnerable within a city? Is it a protection *from* the tyranny of a majority prone to exploit vulnerable communities (Attoh 2011)? Who receives the right to the city (Harvey 2008; Marcuse 2009)? Is a "politics of inhabitants" discriminatory towards the vulnerable (Purcell 2002, 100)?

A key element of the right to the city is that those who live in a city have a right to power within it. But that power has the potential to both empower and discriminate. Because the right to the city is based upon where one lives, it inherits the bias and discrimination that plays into the geography of *who* lives *where* in a city. Ladson-Billings and Tate (1995) argue that housing is foundational for understanding racism within cities. They argue that society is based upon property rights and that property rights have historically been racialized. The right to the city challenges such a perspective by shifting power from those who own property to those who live in a city. But such a right is subject to the same pressures that cause housing segregation. Discrimination and bias in housing policy play a dual role: they make it more difficult for people of color to live in certain communities, but historically they have also contributed to locking people of color out of the wealth gains that come with owning property. Thus, discrimination both locks communities of color out of certain neighborhoods and contributes to communities of color being less likely to be able to afford middle-class neighborhoods. Since the right to the city is grounded in (informal) residency, it is subject to the historical and present-day pressures that contribute to de facto segregation.

Essentially, the right to the city functions in the context of both what Friedman (1969) calls structural racism and what Feagin (2014) calls systemic racism. Racism is structural in the ways that policies have excluded city residents from ownership, or more recently, have discriminated in mortgage practices. It is systemic in that racism also works in soft ways, not through formal policies but through implicit bias and allegedly race-neutral policies that have racial effects. Alexander (2010) lays out the damage these policies do to black communities. It should be no surprise that the same forces are at play in the right to the city. In fact, systemic racism may be particularly powerful at the neighborhood and resident level. Bonilla-Silva (2010) argues that "abstract liberalism," which explains racial differences using political liberalism (equal opportunity) and economic liberalism (individualism) is particularly powerful in communities seeking to explain why exclusion is not racist. Such explanations often lean on cultural explanations: if a community only had a better culture, its individuals would take advantage of "equal opportunity." These explanations are also deeply embedded in the logic of community. The same language of protecting neighborhoods is used to oppose predatory development *and* to actively oppose programs such as busing to integrate schools. Bonilla-Silva argues that abstract liberalism and color-blindness can actually reaffirm structural and systemic racism; the logic of maintaining communities that are themselves the result of structural and systemic racism can reaffirm divides in similar ways. It is little surprise that neighborhood movements such as that found in New Orleans, which embraces the place and community elements of the right to the city, might be subject to similar challenges. The very informality they use to fight more organized political forces within and outside the city might contribute to a "tyranny of structurelessness," which allows specific individuals to overwhelm and control the informal group (Freeman 1972, 151).

It is here that the post-Katrina context is particularly important – that context highlights and sharpens the global conditions that underpin the right to the city and is the impetus for the neighborhood movement catching fire. On August 29, 2005, Hurricane Katrina hit New Orleans. The resulting flood would eventually result in $60 billion in damages (Birkland 2006). It had been eerily predicted by a feature in *National Geographic* (Bourne 2004), which explained how the city's infrastructure for addressing flooding during a hurricane could fail and strand many of the city's most vulnerable residents.

The failures of the disaster recovery effort by the Federal Emergency Management Agency (FEMA) have been catalogued by many researchers (Daniels 2007). Naomi Klein (2007) famously called what happened in New Orleans after Hurricane Katrina "disaster capitalism," a form of capitalism that uses disasters to shift to privatization, even favoring politically connected firms. But such control in New Orleans was not limited to disaster recovery. Many aspects of the public sector were shifted dramatically without democratic control, including a shift to a school district almost entirely made up of charter schools. Simultaneously, residents struggled to return to the city or start to rebuild their houses or neighborhoods. Poised just before the social media explosion, many neighbors did not have any way to reach one another. Their return posed a chicken and egg problem; infrastructure would not be returned until enough residents were back, but residents individually were hesitant to return without clarity about when or whether their infrastructure would return. I saw this up close in a school facilities meeting; there, public officials explained the challenge of figuring out how many and which schools would open when they did not know how many residents would return to various neighborhoods. Residents faced the opposite challenge. Without knowing what schools would open, it was difficult to commit to moving back to the city. This song and dance played out over various utilities. As we will see throughout this text, issues as diverse as mail delivery and potholes impeded the neighborhoods' struggles to recovery.

Neighborhood associations became a natural way to address these issues, and the natural location of a politics of inhabitants. Residents used them to connect and coordinate their returns and then to coordinate advocacy to ensure their neighborhoods received services. At the same time, political leaders were struggling to reach a different (and as we will discuss, whiter) voting population. This would eventually lead to the first white city council and first white mayor in decades. Neighborhood associations became a way to reach difficult-to-contact voting populations, empowering them further.

Amidst this local organizing, a particular language of resistance was developing. Public housing advocates, facing the potential closure of multiple public housing projects despite minimal flood or wind damage, adopted the language of the "right of return" to ensure that public housing residents would have a chance to return to their homes once rebuilt – something uncommon with many Hope VI-style rebuilds, where lower-density housing was emphasized. Johnson

(2011a) argues that while the right to the city banner was never lifted in New Orleans, the adoption of the "right of return" motto framed the public housing debate and was indicative of a wider embrace of elements of the right to the city.

This politics of insiders vs. outsiders and of localism came to define much of the first few years after Hurricane Katrina. The global, neoliberal pressure on cities (Harvey 2012) put a crushing pressure on New Orleans's attempts to rebuild, with neighborhood activists responding by pushing back against privatization, the lack of local rights, and a broader sense that being a resident should mean having more influence.

King, Keohane, and Verba (1984, 43) argue that "social science should tell us something about classes of events as well as about specific events in a particular place." In this case, New Orleans is also a critical test case for understanding both a type of neighborhood movement that is likely to appear in other cities and what happens when such a movement embraces elements of the right to the city. Mayer (2009) highlights the gaps between theory on the right to the city and the way movements practice such theory. In practice, these movements might negatively affect certain racial groups or vulnerable populations (Purcell 2008) or be taken advantage of by the already powerful and coerced (see Harvey 2008 and Marcuse 2009). Post-Katrina New Orleans provides a particularly powerful case for an examination of these issues. Many studies on the right to the city focus explicitly on individual activism campaigns. New Orleans provides the context for a comparative study because elements of the right to the city movement – particularly this insider vs. outsider lens pervasive to post-Katrina New Orleans – were embraced throughout the city. That was true on a policy level, where a wide spectrum of policies was overhauled, but also on a neighborhood level, where a variety of different neighborhoods with differing demographics engaged in activism as well. At the policy level, New Orleanians saw education adopt system-changing policies such as open enrollment (in which residents were no longer committed to sending their children to the school in their community) and an influx of charter schools managed not by the school district but by largely nonprofit charter management organizations. Housing saw a similar shift, with public housing demolished and replaced by less dense housing, rising rental costs as the city experienced a bohemian renaissance, and an increase in short-term rental companies such as AirBnB putting additional pressure on rents. In the health care sector, there was a shift towards a research hospital model. Charity Hospital (which served much of the New Orleans population, so much so that the moniker a "charity baby" was one of pride) was closed in favor of a bio-medical district linked to Louisiana State University. The research focus was paired with an increase in the number of health clinics to be located directly in neighborhoods, although after an initial burst of success, grant money for this model dried up, leaving significant challenges for the communities left behind.

These types of shifts extended in almost every direction. In transportation, an additional trolley-care was planned for North Rampart Street (the border of the tourist-focused French Quarter), and Providence Housing (a spin-off of Catholic Charities designed to do economic development) commissioned a study to investigate tearing down the I-10, the highway that had sliced through the heart of Tremé, the African-American business district and one of the oldest communities of free blacks in the country. For policy wonks, it was a dream come true, the opportunity to rethink systems in real time without dealing with path dependency. Normally, the infrastructure costs alone of shifting these policies would have made them non-starters. But with millions of dollars in water damage across the city (paid out by the Federal Emergency Management Agency or covered by flood insurance), policy-makers had the opportunity to widen the scope of their imagination. Residents were more worried. Many of these decisions were made without democratic input. Residents predictably argued that *their school* and *their hospital* should reopen. Squabbles erupted about proposed changes. The jazz-conscious Tremé community, for example, pointed out that many second lines (unique New Orleans parades with marching brass bands, often after the death of a prominent community member) had routes under the highway and that many iconic moments – such as residents dancing on top of cars – took place under the highway. These smaller arguments blossomed in the context of a wider angst of an insider vs outsider politics in which local neighborhood associations came to represent localism.

Such a density of examples of this politics of inhabitants provides a critical context for comparison, something lacking both in our understanding of neighborhood movements and in the empirical right to the city studies that tends to focus on specific cases, not comparative ones. Neighborhoods and their priorities can be contrasted, each working within the same wider state and political context, as well as within the specific post-Katrina context. So often, movements embracing the right to the city or its ethos are studied in isolation, while attempts at comparison across regions and cultures suffer because context and mores differ so widely or comparisons are made of large social movements across eras (see Polletta 2002). New Orleans thus provides an opportunity to examine a wide variety of movements, across neighborhoods and policy issues but within the same general context. The post-Katrina context is a natural experiment of sorts, with multiple neighborhoods engaging in a similar politics across racial divides, cultural divides, and policy divides.

This research uses these cases within the New Orleans context to address key challenges for neighborhood movements, such as whether such movements reinforce justice or reinforce existing power dynamics. Put simply, if neighborhoods are empowered, will this brand of politics improve the plight of vulnerable communities or undermine them?

There is a robust discussion in the right to the city literature around these specific questions. For de Souza (2001), the right to the city is a response to oppression and exploitation in cities, which keeps vulnerable residents from taking advantage of the beauty that cities have to offer. De Souza highlights the participatory planning movement as an opportunity for residents to address oppression and ensure an ideal city. In particular, the right to the city is a tool to ensure social justice, particularly when it comes to housing arrangements in Brazil, where residents addressed slums and informal housing where vulnerable populations had few rights.

De Souza (2001) recognizes critiques of participatory budgeting and the right to the city more broadly, acknowledging that neighborhood leaders may not have appropriate knowledge, that participation can be inefficient, and that people may only know what's best for their neighborhood, not the broader city. But despite acknowledging that movements such as the right to the city are not a panacea, de Souza argues that the right to the city and participatory budgeting are critical tools in the fight for social justice.

In summing up this argument, Herbert (2005, 853) writes that "given the hallowed nature of localized democratic action, projects that foreground community presumably possess great legitimacy." But he continues to argue that, in doing so, "[s]tates can thus ostensibly off-load responsibilities to communities with minimal political cost because this can be legitimated as strengthening local control." This is the first of several sharp critiques around justice issues applicable to neighborhood movements. Historically, the Catholic Church has defined "social justice" by arguing that "[s]ociety ensures social justice when it provides the conditions that allow associations or individuals to obtain what is their due, according to their nature and their vocation. Social justice is linked to the common good and the exercise of authority" (Rhonheimer 2015, 47). Rawls (2001) takes a simpler approach to justice, arguing that justice is fairness as represented both by basic liberties and by equal opportunity. Rawls (1965) addresses social justice in his review of Brandt's (1962) edited volume *Social Justice* and points to Frankena's (1962) link to natural law as a foundation for justice itself. Miller (1999) argues that social justice is historically important while being theoretically poorly defined. He attempts to crystallize social justice as focusing on the concepts of desert, need, and equality, but argues that these the definitions are dependent on social context and vary with those contexts. While Brandt, Rawls, and Miller focus primarily on the *justice* elements of social justice, Lake (2017) builds upon Latour's conception of the *social* (2005) to argue that social justice is not just a subset of justice but the relational aspect of all justice. Lake (2017) focuses on injustices that occurred when Camden, NJ, was being developed, specifically highlighting the ways that developers ignored, discredited, and disallowed local input. This last conception of social justice is particularly applicable to neighborhood movements in that it addresses the ways communities can be discriminated against, face inequality, and struggle to meet their needs, and it calls for a means to address these inequities.

Contrary to de Souza's assertion that a politics of inhabitants would improve social justice, Herbert argues that moving power to residents is often a form of neoliberal offloading in which the state receives political cover for providing fewer services. Herbert's concern stands in sharp contrast to the broader conceptualization of the right to the city as seen by such major theorists as Harvey (2008) and Purcell (2006), who see such local democratic action as a counterbalance to or even a conflicting force against a neoliberal expansion. Instead, Herbert argues that investing political power in local communities has a perverse result, diminishing services and putting the burden on local communities to provide them. Thus, the power of such politics to impact economic justice positively is questioned.

In the same way that Herbert (2005) challenges the claim by de Souza (2001) and others that participatory institutions that emphasize the right to the city can serve economic justice, Purcell (2006) challenges the idea that such initiatives can serve democratic justice. Nylen (2003, 120) argues that neoliberalism can be opposed "by setting up participatory instruments of nonelite empowerment and public accountability both inside and outside the state." But Purcell (2006, 1921–2) argues that "localisation can lead to a more democratic city, or a less democratic one. It depends on the agenda of those empowered by a given scalar strategy. The paper does not reject the local scale, therefore; it argues that we should reject the *local trap*." In so arguing, Purcell provides examples of localism movements that did just the opposite, stripping people of rights, with the most extreme example in the United States being the combination of states' rights and slavery. Purcell provides a critical warning that decisions of scale – that is, at what level should democratic decisions be made – need not necessarily lead to democratically just outcomes. Thus, just as a devolution of power from a central government to states viciously stripped democratic justice and the rights of African-Americans by upholding slavery, there are no guarantees that devolution to the neighborhood level ultimately leads to democratic justice within cities.

Purcell's (2006) example of slavery in the US South highlights not only democratic justice, but also racial justice. Just as empowering local neighborhoods in urban communities has the potential to undermine economic justice and democratic justice, it also has the potential to undermine racial justice (Purcell 2002). A key element of the right to the city is that the breadth of the slogan makes it applicable across a wide spectrum of situations. Thus, participatory budgeting in Brazil can be seen as a manifestation of the right to the city, just as the fight for slums rights in Mexico (Adler 2015) can be. But theorists such as Harvey (2012, xv) argue that this malleability also means the mantle can be adopted by those already in power because "the right to the city is an empty signifier. Everything depends on who gets to fill it with meaning. The financiers and developers can claim it, and have every right to do so. But then, so can the homeless and *sans-papiers*." Marcuse (2009, 191) sees the same issue but argues that the right to the city must be limited:

> It's crucially important to be clear that it is not everyone's right to the city with which we are concerned, but that there is in fact

a conflict among rights that need to be faced and resolved, rather than wished away. Some already have the right to the city, are running it now, have it well in hand (although "well" might not be just the right word, today!). They are the financial powers, the real estate owners and speculators, the key political hierarchy of state power, the owners of the media.

Marcuse (2009) continues to argue that discontent if not carefully curated can lead to a host of anti-justice positions, including anti-abortion, guns, anti-tax, homophobia, religious fundamentalism, war-mongering, family values, false patriotism, sports fanaticism, and "homeownership as the American Dream" (Marcuse 2009, 192). Alongside these positions, discontent can also lead to racism and anti-immigrant sentiment (ibid.). Herbert (2005, 858) examines what these biases look like when it comes to renters:

> As one renter said, explaining why he and his fellow renters were uninvolved in neighborhood politics, "Well, why should we be? Because we're renters! It's not like we own any of this. There's no pride in renting something." Said another, accentuating his anticipation of a short term in his neighborhood, "[Y]ou don't want to invest in a car that you know is going to break down sooner or later. Sooner or later, I'm going to be leaving, so I'm not going to put money into it." Homeowners evinced a similarly dismissive attitude toward the possibilities of organizing renters. Frequently, renters were derided not just for their apathy, but for being inattentive to the properties they occupied and for failing to engage in productive neighboring. Said one homeowner, "[Y]ou go into a renter's house, it's just disgusting filth. Just disgusting." Renters are thus symbolically suspect (Perin 1977), even unclean (Douglas 1991), and thus stand as a seemingly insurmountable impediment to organizing those neighborhoods where their presence is extensive.

These critiques are particularly pertinent to neighborhood politics. Herbert (2005, 861–2) argues that

> [e]ven those who were content in their middle-class neighborhood harbored fears that those yet more affluent were consistently better favored. One resident, for example, referred to what

he termed the "lunatic fringe" – the very wealthy who lived on the top of a bluff above his property – and their ability to get what they want. Those in less-advantaged areas often described a sense of stigma emanating from the city officials with whom they dealt, a castigation of their neighborhood as simply undeserving. This made it easier, they believed, for their requests to be refused.

As we will see in New Orleans, neighborhood renters often sit at the intersection of race and class divides. Ladson-Billings and Tate (2005) argue that housing both historically and presently is power-fully shaped by race and racism. The exclusion of blacks from legally owning property, discrimination against blacks (and Latinos) through zoning and red-lining, and, later, the use of predatory loans that both contributed to the 2008 market crash and preyed specifically on com-munities of color; all contribute to systemic racism. They also con-tribute to the linking of race and renters – the same way that welfare was pathologized by stereotyping black women. Bonilla-Silva (2010) argues that these links allow a surface of color-blindness while per-mitting discrimination to continue. Feagin (2014) makes a softer claim that such biases may be implicit. Active discrimination and implicit bias that act against people of color seeking to move to (or rent in) a community are challenges for the right to the city and its claim to seek justice. For Herbert (2005, 858), "community thus emerges as a suspect political project because it balkanizes the population and enables the better organized to prosper at the expense of those who are less advantaged." Purcell (2002), similarly, argues that too often when discussing community, local working classes are conflated with those who hold anti-racist or anti-capitalist views. Yet, working-class identity politics can often work in the opposite direction, with financial insecurity being funneled into racial or anti-immigrant animus. In other words, focusing on local empowerment may undermine, not improve, racial justice.

Purcell (2002, 100) argues that "it is disconcerting because we can-not know what kind of a city these new urban politics will produce." Neighborhood empowerment is often seen as a salve to address such injustices, but theorists argue that movements such as the right to the city could undermine the very issues they attempt to address.

That such issues would come up in the post-Katrina New Orleans context was inevitable. In perhaps the starkest example, Arena (2012) argues that the movement to oppose the demolition of public housing was ultimately undercut by nonprofit partners that had too much at stake with funders to be seen as radical. In keeping with sharp critiques of the nonprofit sector more widely, Arena argues that the nature of the sector undermines calls for government to provide services, because nonprofit partners are unable to critique government while depending on government for funding. These power struggles were played out across policy issues and neighborhoods. They were a dominant theme of the post-Katrina context and the neighborhood movement that emerged from that context. Economic, democratic, and racial values were often in tension, and neighborhoods throughout the city attempted to become involved.

Conducting research on neighborhood associations is almost as messy as the work of the associations themselves, and this study of the New Orleans neighborhood movement is no exception. Research on New Orleans neighborhoods poses distinct challenges, from rigor to access and ethics.

Neighborhood associations are largely absent from research on New Orleans. They appear as a protest agent in Ford's (2010) *The Trouble with City Planning*, where the Broadmoor Improvement Association, New Orleans's most famous neighborhood association, plays a brief role. In that telling, the association opposes the Urban Land Institute's plan for the city's recovery. Similarly, neighborhood associations appear around the edges in a pair of works about the push towards privatization in New Orleans after Hurricane Katrina (Arena 2012; Adams 2013).

In Arena (2013), neighborhood associations appeared only in a not-in-my-backyard role in fighting to demolish public housing. Adams (2013, 158) also frames neighborhood associations in terms of privatization, arguing that

> [o]rganizations like the Broadmoor Improvement Association have been extraordinarily successful in garnering public recognition and price-sector funding from foundations, charities, and philanthropies. They have protected and rebuilt communities that were essentially slated for abandonment. These groups reveal a sense of ongoing antagonism and mistrust of local and regional government, and they embrace the private sector as a radical and plentiful alternative to what they see as the social, governmental neglect of the poor and under-resourced sectors of the city. In other words, these types of organizations are a response to what are seen as governmental failures to protect citizens. Rather than

calling for better governmental policies, these groups are turning to the private sector to solve their problems.

In each of these pieces of research, neighborhood associations play a supplementary role to a wider ideological point – neighborhood associations are not the focus of such research, but rather bit actors in a wider discourse on neoliberalism, privatization, and participation. Other authors make neighborhood associations central actors in their research, but do so by focusing on success stories. Chamlee-Wright (2008) and Chamlee-Wright and Storr (2009) focus on the most successful neighborhood associations as supports for libertarian ideals of limited government, reflecting the influence of the libertarian Mercatus Center, which became involved in the city after the storm. Hummel and Ahlers (2007) partnered directly with the Broadmoor Improvement Association in an effort to create a model for neighborhood recovery.

From Adams (2013) and Ford (2010) to Chamlee-Wright (2008) and Hummel and Ahlers (2007), the one constant is the use of the Broadmoor Improvement Association to prove wider ideological points. For Adams (2013), neighborhood associations confirm the danger of incentives to divest responsibilities from government and privatize governance. For Chamlee-Wright (2008), the Broadmoor Improvement Association is an example of how local communities can bind together to fulfill what might otherwise be governmental duties – a key tenet of libertarianism. This language was even adopted by a local nonprofit, City-Works (2008), which called the city's elite neighborhood associations "pseudo-governments."

Such an approach ignores a key potential problem with case study research. What if the selected case is not representative of the wider population of neighborhood associations? Indeed, as I will discuss in more detail in Chapter 2, Broadmoor is a highly atypical neighborhood. Among the irregularities is the involvement of Harvard University, which adopted the neighborhood and helped it plan its post-disaster strategy. But having the support of a prominent university in fundraising, planning, and research is highly atypical of such associations. To make a single association – one that receives atypical support from a world-class university – the heart of a new governance model or a new model for disaster relief seems tenuous at best.

Thus, the first challenge for the study of neighborhood associations is how to create rigor in sampling neighborhood associations. In Appendix I, I lay out the ways in which rigor is closely linked to access and community involvement. That appendix argues that rigorous qualitative research requires understanding community context and collaborating with community members. Community involvement allows for both the access necessary to compile a rich qualitative data set, and also the context and knowledge necessary for effective qualitative analysis. In this research, even creating a sample frame was challenging. There was no authoritative list of neighborhood associations, making traditional sampling techniques difficult. Community groups had the same problem, in fact, the city council officers I contacted were so eager for an updated list of neighborhood association contacts that they made me promise to share my findings.

The first step to a rigorous study was to create a sampling frame – something I did in collaboration with the small and now-defunct nonprofit City-Works. The nonprofit had conducted a census of neighborhood organizations (City-Works 2008) after the storm – though the study was not usable for academic purposes. I partnered with them and reproduced the survey (see City-Works 2010 and Appendix I). The result was both a sampling frame and baseline survey data on organizations such as membership, budget, priorities, and boundaries.

Because so much of the writing on New Orleans neighborhood associations (and on the right to the city more broadly) focuses on single cases with big accomplishments, I used a sample that stratified the overall budget. That ensured that the study included small, harder to contact neighborhood associations as well as larger, well-oiled associations. I drew a total of 15 associations across five categories – four different budgetary levels and one category for associations that chose not to answer the budget question. Two associations refused to take part in the study (additional associations were redrawn into their stratum), while a third eventually dropped out of the study after agreeing to participate. The remaining 14 associations are introduced in detail in Chapter 2, but they spanned New Orleans geographically and demographically.

I used a variety of methods to study each association: survey data, participant observation, interviews, and document analysis (of meeting minutes). Individuals were kept anonymous, but neighborhoods and organizations were not. The goal in working across these methods was to provide a well-rounded perspective on what associations do – that is, to understand this neighborhood movement through specific actions and logics within associations and their leaders, and in doing so to move away from simplifying assumptions about community. Leading with the empirical cases, and more specifically with *what associations do,* had the dual effect of providing structure to conversations with activists about informal associations that can drift into difficult-to-confirm rumors, as well as providing the platform for a comparative examination that shows the ways neighborhood movements embrace and ignore elements of the right to the city. The methods blended multiple perspectives, avoided leaning too heavily on the activist, and provided cross-references for events and memories. Repeatedly spending time in the city served a similar purpose, ensuring that the relationships I had with local residents and activists were strong enough to help me understand and interpret the data I was collecting. Such feedback is critical because of the challenges faced by young (often white) researchers conducting ethnography in communities of color (see Duncan 2002). Each association was the site of two interviews of leaders within the association, and a third interview was conducted with a neighborhood's key partner. These interviews focused on the major actions of an association, then cross-referenced with meeting minutes, observation from association meetings, and other public meetings throughout the city.

The result is a comparative analysis that moves beyond simplifying assumptions about community or single cases of using the right to the city as a slogan to a deep examination of the New Orleans neighborhood movement and the ways in which it embraces elements of the right to the city while rejecting others. This study of New Orleans and its neighborhood associations is the first of its kind that specifically compares the actions that result from a politics of inhabitants, and does so across demographic and geographic lines within a controlled political environment, essentially creating an embedded case model. Each association is embedded within the wider New Orleans political context, which embraced the ethos of the right to the city in response to policy changes after Hurricane Katrina. Within each association there are several embedded "actions," each constructed in this text from triangulating survey data, interview data, document analysis, and observation. See Figure 1.1.

The rich blend of sixty-six cases of neighborhood action across fourteen neighborhoods provides the groundwork for an investigation that can empirically address the justice concerns that dot the landscape of the right to the city. The results are messy and contradictory. Some

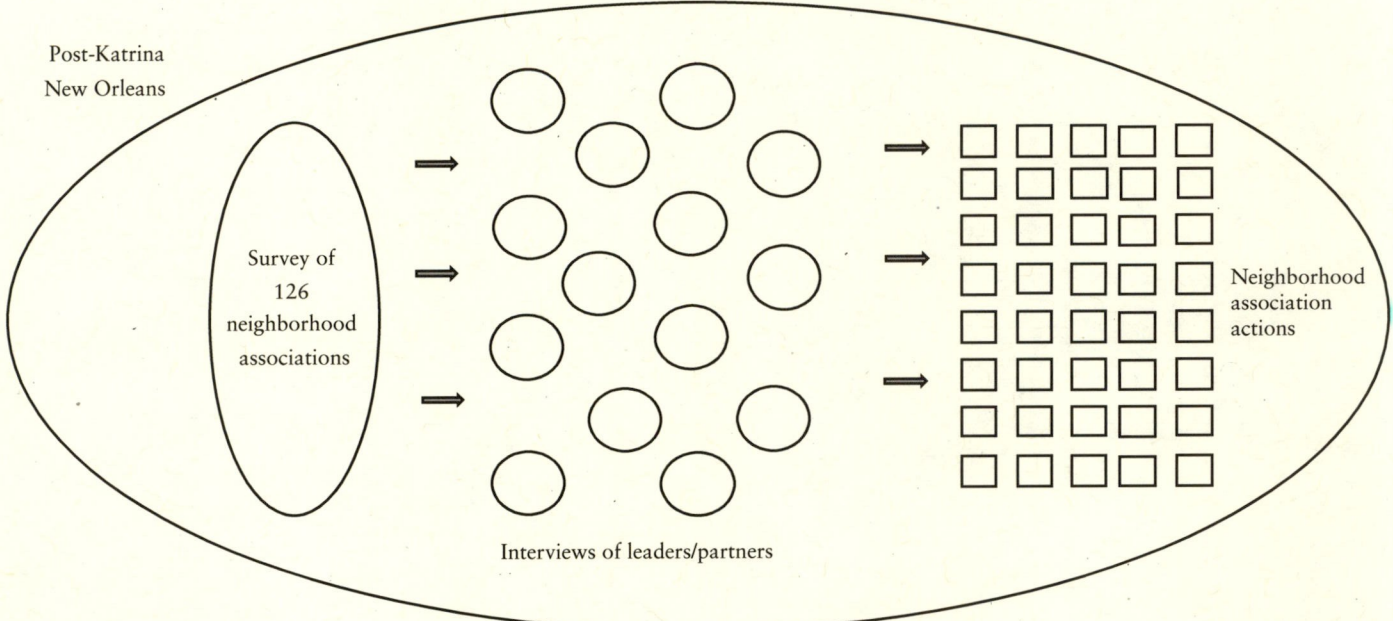

Figure 1.1 Embedded case study
Within New Orleans, the study surveyed 126 associations, conducted 42 interviews within a sample of 14 associations, and analyzed hundreds of neighborhood actions.

associations specifically fight for justice and vulnerable populations. Others are based upon a logic that focuses on property values and excludes those who they worry might cause those values to dip. Most have democratic infrastructure, although elections end up being far less important than volunteering, and burnout far more important than votes. And for each empowering opportunity that crosses racial lines, NIMBYism threatens to draw the lines in sharpie.

The world of these quirky neighborhood associations is a messy one. Their goals are often contradictory and the outcomes even more so. For these neighborhood leaders, the right to the city is a tenuous right, and its pursuit has both victories and casualties.

◆

2

The Neighborhood:
A Neoliberal Contradiction

I always thought that the city after Katrina came back largely on the back of the associations.

Twain, president of the Fontainebleau Improvement Association

We don't have time to deal with intractable social issues.

Louise, executive director of the Vieux Carré Property Owners, Residents, and Associates

The New Orleans neighborhood movement that grew out of the post-Katrina insider/outsider political angst shares the international challenge of cities facing fiscal pressure from a globalized economy: the need for a people's movement as a counterbalance to the interests of developers. New Orleans faces tremendous pressure from both gentrification and tourism. In this, it has much in common with cities across the world. David Harvey (2012) addresses these tensions, arguing that investment leads to a Disneyfication that converts cities from places where people can live to artificial theme parks where the rich play. Harvey (2012, 104–5) uses Barcelona as an example, writing:

> Barcelona's initial success appears to be headed deep into the first contradiction. As opportunities to pocket monopoly rents galore present themselves on the basis of the collective symbolic capital of Barcelona as a city (property prices have skyrocketed since the Roal Institute of Architects awarded the whole city its medal for architectural accomplishments), so their irresistible lure draws more and more homogenizing multinational commodification

in its wake. The later phases of waterfront development look exactly like every other in the western world: the stupefying congestion of the traffic leads to pressures to put boulevards through parts of the cold city, multinational stores replace local shops, gentrification removes long-term residential populations and destroys older urban fabric, and Barcelona loses some of its marks of distinction. There are even unsubtle signs of Disneyfication.

Jane Jacobs (1961) notes the same struggle in city neighborhoods, arguing that the cheap rents and opportunities for local entrepreneurship draw artists and customers. But, as a neighborhood becomes more and more successful using this model, rents increase, chains and homogenous shops enter, and eventually the distinctiveness of the block or neighborhood gives way to a monotony that can no longer attract consumers.

In New Orleans, this fear is real, particularly in downtown neighborhoods. As Harvey (2012, 104) notes, in Barcelona or in cities such as Paris, Athens, Rio de Janeiro, Berlin, and Rome, the distinctiveness of the city is in part what makes it a destination (he compares these cities to Baltimore, Liverpool, Essen, Lille, and Glasgow, which do not have quite as much "symbolic capital"). But, the process of building on the reputation of such cities creates tension with the very things that support it. In Barcelona, the city's character abets investment, but new investment along the waterfront does not share that same character. Thus, the waterfront is at once only possible because of Barcelona's beautiful boulevards and iconic quality of life, but the waterfront development threatens to undermine that very character and beauty. Similarly, in New Orleans, big-ticket items designed to attract tourists, such as Harrah's casino, stand out like sore thumbs and threaten to undermine the character of downtown neighborhoods such as the French Quarter. There are two dangers here: the first is that the city loses its character, but the second is the threat of Disneyfication – that the character ceases to be alive and becomes a caricature of what made it distinctive. In this scenario, the French Quarter would no longer be a thriving, historical neighborhood full of art and artists, but rather a sterile tourist attraction commemorating that such a neighborhood once existed. That can happen in various ways, from regulation, to development, to simply putting the needs of tourists above those of residents.

The wider discussion of Disneyfication is a manifestation both of capitalism, as Harvey (2012) argues, but also of the ways that neo-liberalism manifests as the market's drive to commodify and eventually undermine neighborhood uniqueness. The New Orleans neighborhood movement rose specifically to challenge this trend. Purcell (2002) argues that a *politics of inhabitants* might play a similar role in cities, making decisions about space and development and counterbalancing capitalism and global neoliberal pressures. That vision of the right to the city as a tool to counterbalance market forces in development is being adopted among other scholars of social movements (see Balzarini and Shlay 2016).

Neighborhood associations provide a potential tool for such a counterbalance, and the New Orleans neighborhood movement provides the opportunity to understand the ways such a counterbalance might fit into neighborhood politics – there is no guarantee that the counterbalance would adopt the specifically anti-capitalist framework advocated by Harvey (2012). Logan and Rabrenovic (1990, 68) theorize that "for our purposes, a neighborhood association is defined as a civic organization oriented toward maintaining or improving the quality of life in a geographically delimited residential area." Austin (1991, 516) adds that neighborhood associations range from loosely knit organizations to highly formalized ones with written rules and procedures, and participation spans a wide range of levels. These definitions identify three key traits of neighborhood associations: (1) an organization dedicated to improving the quality of life; (2) an organization that serves a geographically delimited residential area; and (3) wide discrepancies in formality and participation among organizations. The focus by such associations on participatory rights that come from *living in a community* overlaps with most conceptions of the right to the city, as does the concept that such neighborhood associations might provide a counterbalance to the forces of developers. But associations also hold the potential to sharply diverge from the anti-capitalistic ideology of the right to city; neighborhood associations are grounded in property rights, and many of the most vigorous members participate explicitly to ensure that property values increase.

Further, neoliberalism is not limited to development, and neighborhood associations are not limited to opposing development. Herbert (2005) identifies neoliberal offloading as a potential side effect of the localization. In his account, local organizations are not opposing neoliberalism but enabling it. In attempting to garner more power, local organizations allow city government to abdicate its responsibilities. The result is that the burden for providing services falls increasingly on local communities without the resources to perform them adequately. Local leaders are then crushed with the added burden of providing services that previously were or should have been provided by municipalities.

It is here that our specific conversation about New Orleans starts – at the intersection of local power and service provision. After Hurricane Katrina, spunky neighborhood associations became central to the city's political climate. The perception of neighborhood associations as powerful has an origin myth, one that vastly overestimates the strength of these associations. A second myth came with political allure: the city saw an opportunity to offload provision of services to neighborhood associations, using the logic of localism to try to create the holy grail of politics – cheaper and better services. As it turns out, both myths are fatally flawed, and their flaws require a reconfiguration of our understanding of the relationship between neighborhood associations and neoliberalism.

In New Orleans, the origin myth of neighborhood associations possessing profound power starts with the story of the Broadmoor Improvement Association, an organization with tremendous power and the capacity to provide neighborhood services. Understanding Broadmoor as a myth, why that myth matters, and how misleading that myth is as a metaphor when in the context of other associations' experiences requires extensive local context. Much of the controversy following Hurricane Katrina was over failed attempts by the Federal Emergency Management Agency to serve residents who had not evacuated, or who had returned to the city (Sobel and Leeson 2006). But the city also faced a daunting longer-term set of challenges. New Orleans residents developed their own shorthand to describe the difference. The issues of life and death immediately following the storm, such as evacuating the remaining residents from roofs or surviving in the Superdome while waiting for help, were called disaster response. "Recovery" referred to longer-term challenges, such as which schools, hospitals, and public housing projects should be allowed to reopen. But before recovery even began, the Speaker of the House, Dennis Hastert, and a prominent University of Pennsylvania academic (Foster and Giegengack 2006) were calling for New Orleans to be moved to another location, while the consensus of planners was that the footprint of the city needed to be reduced (Ford 2010). This footprint referred to the areas in which people lived across New Orleans. The idea to limit population to those areas safest and least likely to flood was rooted in the city's history. The city's earliest development had been along what is commonly known as the "sliver by the river," a narrow, natural levy that was the result of sediment from the flooding of the Mississippi River (Horne 2008). The sliver by the river did not flood, even during Hurricane Katrina. Later in the city's history, low-lying lands were filled in and development extended. These communities tended to be poorer and blacker, and were exposed to higher flood risks.

The consensus of planners after Hurricane Katrina was to concentrate development in high-lying areas and move people from the most vulnerable, low-lying areas to the historical heart of the city (Ford 2010). But, in New Orleans, things are never quite that easy. That plan was dead upon arrival in New Orleans, a casualty of the manner in which recovery was pursued at the state level and of the indifference to the struggle of residents returning to the city. Many of the residents who came back to New Orleans found their insurance claims denied; insurers insisted the damage was due to flooding, not the hurricane, and that insurance only covered the latter. The state-run Road Home program, outsourced to a private corporation (Adams 2013), made a catastrophic decision to reimburse residents for rebuilding costs rather than to provide upfront grants. The purpose was to avoid fraud, but the result was to drive many homeowners into bankruptcy. The slow-moving program had so much trouble confirming payment claims that it was referred to locally as the Road to Homelessness. Many residents paid for repairs on short-term loans, confident that reimbursement was in the works, but then lost their homes to foreclosure and declared bankruptcy before they saw any reimbursement.

That was the policy context that the Urban Land Institute, hired to help create a plan for New Orleans's revival, entered into. The firm was hired by the Bring New Orleans Back Commission to produce a blueprint for the city's recovery. The blueprint was in line with urban planning recommendations, including a reduced city footprint. Yet, the Urban Land Institute's blueprint also was tone-deaf to the needs of the residents. This plan, infamously referred to as the Green Dot Plan (see Figure 2.1), turned dangerously low-lying

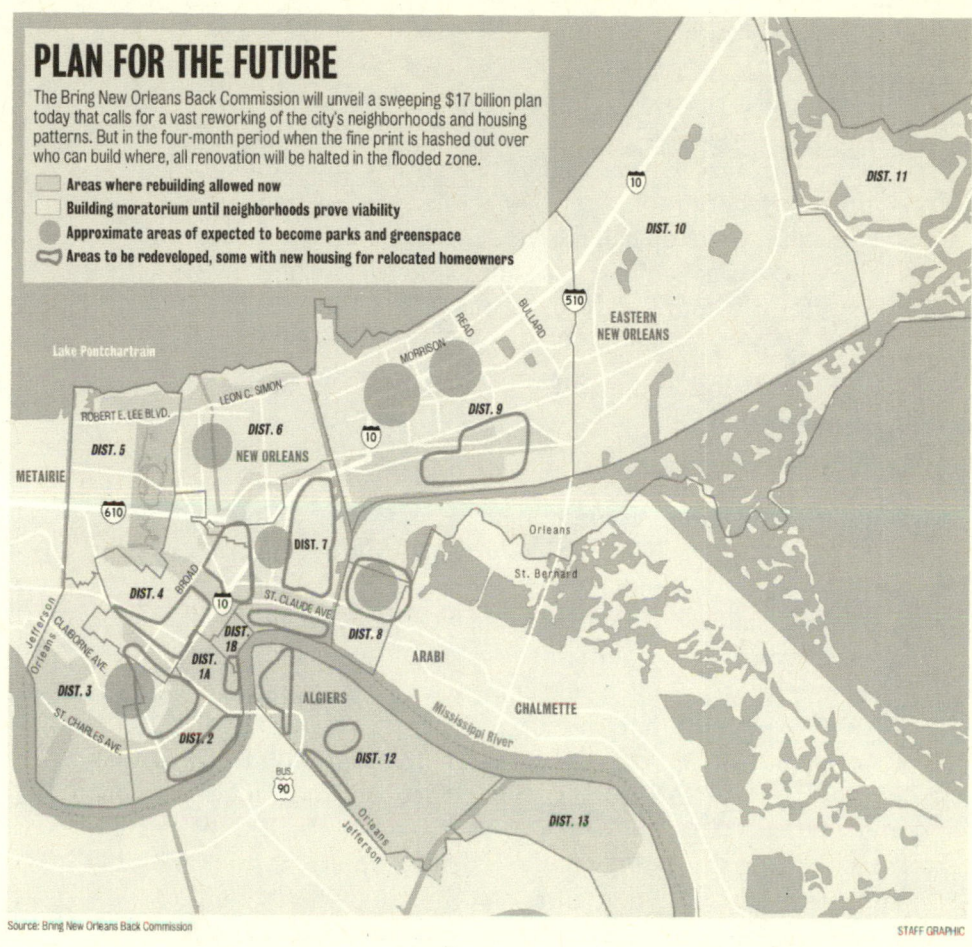

PLAN FOR THE FUTURE

The Bring New Orleans Back Commission will unveil a sweeping $17 billion plan today that calls for a vast reworking of the city's neighborhoods and housing patterns. But in the four-month period when the fine print is hashed out over who can build where, all renovation will be halted in the flooded zone.

- Areas where rebuilding allowed now
- Building moratorium until neighborhoods prove viability
- Approximate areas of expected to become parks and greenspace
- Areas to be redeveloped, some with new housing for relocated homeowners

Source: Bring New Orleans Back Commission

STAFF GRAPHIC

Figure 2.1 Green Dot map
The map that set off the controversy over neighborhood involvement in recovery.
Courtesy of Karen Gadbois.

neighborhoods into parks designed to help the city contain flooding. The neighborhoods marked with green dots were destined to become those parks.

Green Dot was, on its surface, modern, reasonable, and viable. From the perspective of urban planners puzzled that the city had extended development into low-lying communities, it was a path to a more sensible city with fewer residents living in areas with a high flood risk. But the public reaction was swift and negative. Residents were already risking bankruptcy to return to their homes and here was a plan that suggested they be evacuated *en masse* and permanently relocated. Gratz (2015, 43) sums up the sentiment against the plan:

> The report was so overreaching, so absent of legitimate local input and disdainful of the democratic process that it served as a startling wake-up call regarding the new elite agenda for the city. And it was only January at this point, less than five months since Katrina and Rita. Clearly, the citizens had no choice but to develop their own battle plans. The report energized nascent local organizations all over town that were ten steps ahead of officials and already jump-starting the process of rebuilding their city.

Mayor Ray Nagin not only walked away from the Green Dot Plan, but walked away from the Bring New Orleans Back Commission as well. To many residents, turning low-lying communities into parks seemed too similar to rumors that New Orleans was to excise its poor, minority communities and use the storm as impetus to gentrify. That idea, that New Orleans would come back whiter and wealthier, was stoked by a rumor that a group of business elites met with Mayor Ray Nagin to do just that (Nagin 2011; Johnson 2011a). Local businessman James Reis became a public advocate for changing the city, arguing that "those who want to see this city rebuilt want to see it done in a completely different way: demographically, geographically and politically" and that elites "would leave the city unless New Orleans improved its services and reduced the number of poor people" (Gratz 2015).

Neighborhoods, fearful of becoming a "green dot" on the map, were convinced they needed to fight for their survival. Even after the mayor rejected the Green Dot Plan, he stoked the flames of neighborhood paranoia by insisting that neighborhoods would have to prove their viability to qualify for public services, and the Lambert Plan, which succeeded Green Dot (but also was never fully enacted), focused on neighborhood plans that sought input from neighborhood organizations. In response, neighborhoods, naturally, started to organize. Foremost among those organizing was the Broadmoor neighborhood.

The Broadmoor Improvement Association existed long before the storm, but when the neighborhood faced extinction as a "green dot," the association quickly became a political force in the city. It partnered with a host of organizations, from Harvard University and Bard College to the Clinton Foundation and the Episcopal Church of the Annunciation. The organization not only advocated for itself at the city level, but also created a neighborhood plan and marshaled the resources to pursue that plan. It reached out to neighbors, encouraging them to return. It surveyed its neighborhood to update residency information. It used Annunciation Church as a hub to bring volunteer labor into the city and apply for a host of grants. Those volunteers gutted houses, mowed lawns, made repairs, and eventually put together a social services division and helped draw a new charter school to the neighborhood. The success of the association, which claims it received millions of dollars of in-kind donations and labor after the storm, was reflected in the political sphere, and the long-time president of the association would eventually win a seat on city council.

Broadmoor quickly became the go-to example of a strident, powerful neighborhood association. City-Works (2008) called it a pseudo-government. The libertarian-leaning Mercatus Institute at George Mason University held up the association as an example of a neighborhood that needed little government assistance (Chamlee-Wright 2008; Chamlee-Wright and Storr, 2009). Inside New Orleans, the success of Broadmoor provided a different lesson. Neighborhoods believed that they needed to bind together to protect themselves and successfully lobby for their fair share of resources. Other neighborhoods feared that the well-organized Broadmoor was taking more than its fair share of resources. They saw the race to avoid becoming a green dot as a zero-sum game and Broadmoor as their competition for both resources and survival. And so the myth of the powerful neighborhood association grew and became a self-fulfilling prophecy. Other neighborhood associations struggled to play catch-up, and residents' participation in associations blew through the roof (City-Works 2008). But, despite increased involvement in these associations, the typical association looked nothing like Broadmoor.

This marked an important departure from the right to the city literature, which tended to be vague about how this right would be pursued while focusing more on its potential impact. In New Orleans, neighborhood associations grounded in a politics of inhabitants had little power or money and faced potential competition for influence. Only a handful of neighborhood associations across the city had paid staff. Of three associations (out of 126) in the census with paid staff, two used the staffer part-time to produce a newsletter – these were not professional organizations. The third was the Broadmoor Improvement Association. Budgets reflected the same reality. Twenty per cent of the associations surveyed reported an annual budget of zero dollars, and that meant that items as simple as a hard copy of an agenda to be handed out at meetings were paid for out of pocket. Forty per cent of associations had budgets under $1,000, and 77 per cent had annual budgets of less than $5,000. Broadmoor refused to answer questions about its budget in the survey, but in later interviews claimed millions of dollars in resources and in-kind donations. Across the city, a small handful of associations (such as Broadmoor and the Lakeview Civic Improvement Association) gathered power, but the average association had few resources. These were not powerhouse organizations. They were not pseudo-governments. They were mom-and-pop shops trying to cobble together donations or member fees so that they could distribute flyers for their annual neighborhood cleanups.

The myth of the neighborhood associations as powerful entities that can replace the function of local government is a flawed one. But, in New Orleans, a second myth grew out of the first. Politicians looked to Broadmoor and trusted that neighborhoods could provide the holy grail of neoliberal politics – cheaper and better social services. This was not the first time citizen participation and grassroots organizations have been considered an illusory magical elixir to solve a critical puzzle for politicians. Public opinion was in favor of services and in favor of balancing the budget. That left politicians in a bind. They were forever seeking to establish improved social services that were also less expensive. Those who found it, or at a minimum, who fostered an illusion of less expensive yet better services, often skyrocketed to success. The search for that elixir was part of what drove the privatization that overtook New Orleans's education (see Buras 2014) and housing (Arena 2012) sectors. But devolving to nonprofits and private corporations required paying them. The prospect of the unpaid contributions of neighborhood associations was a powerful allure for these same politicians. And they were not alone. Both before and after New Orleans, high-profile politicians would look to the volunteer sector to provide public services that were cheaper and better.

President George W. Bush's "Compassionate Conservatism" looked to faith-based initiatives as a means to improve services while lowering costs. Research by Ram Cnaan (2006) and the work of the first head of faith-based initiatives in the White House, John DiIulio (2007), emphasized the critical role that urban congregations and faith-based organizations play in service delivery in urban environments despite the fact that they are often locked out of government dollars. Compassionate Conservatism was designed to improve services by getting faith-based organizations those dollars. Unfortunately, the Bush White House played politics with the initiative, using it as a tool to whip up conservative votes rather than as a bi-partisan consensus by focusing on issues around the hiring and firing of faith-based institutions receiving government grants. That, combined with an increased shift towards national security after 9/11, meant the idea was never tested (ibid.). A decade later, a similar concept took root in the United Kingdom, where the Conservative Party rode their "Big Society" slogan to an electoral victory. The concept behind Big Society is remarkably familiar: volunteerism and local participation could cut costs and improve services (Building Big Society 2010).

New Orleans's neighborhood associations were critically linked to a fundamental neoliberal question: could the network of neighborhood associations that emerged in post-Katrina New Orleans fulfill the promise of cheaper and better services?

City officials in New Orleans did not miss the opportunity to take advantage of the supposed pseudo-governments cropping up in neighborhoods around New Orleans. They created a Neighborhood Engagement Office. In the office's kickoff event, with neighborhood leaders in attendance, they presented their vision: neighborhood associations that would help the city provide services. Kristen, the president of the North Carrollton Neighborhood Association, was clear about what she thought: "it's not in our charter" and "we are all employed full-time." She was not the only person who felt that way. It turns out that neighborhood leaders do not shy away from explaining how ridiculous the idea is. Greg, from the Upper Audubon Association, put it simply: "To me, there's no reason to even be paying taxes if we won't even get basic services." Neighborhood activists just do not describe their associations in terms of service delivery. Instead, words such as "watchdog" dominate the conversation. Kristen said that the purpose of a neighborhood association was "to get the city to do what people were concerned about." Louise, the executive director of the Vieux Carré Property Owners, Residents, and Associates (VCPORA), echoed the sentiment: "We don't have time to deal with intractable social issues."

The activities of the neighborhood associations confirmed this. Meeting minutes showed that neighborhood associations almost never engaged in the provision of social services. Instead, they focused on beautification and crime, supporting local institutions, and creating social capital. Unlike religious institutions, which serve meals at soup kitchens and often provide housing or other services for low-income residents, neighborhood associations stayed away from service delivery.

This is a first peek into how the New Orleans neighborhood movement interacted with the broader challenge of neoliberal fiscal pressures within the city. The experience of neighborhood associations, both the outlier experience of the Broadmoor Improvement Association and the more common experiences of the other associations in this sample, show that such power is contested and that a politics of inhabitants can transform into a politics of competition in which inhabitants are set against one another in competition for scarce resources. Similarly, Herbert's (2005) frame of offloading was altered in New Orleans for a simple reason: neighborhood associations refused to play along. It was an important moment for the trajectory of the politics of inhabitants in New Orleans because it showed that this movement would stick to an ideology of prioritizing geographical interest, not filling service gaps. It is a critical moment for this study as well, because it breaks the one-size-fits-all nature of the neoliberal critiques of such associations or the one-size-fits-all assertions that such politics would confront neoliberalism. In New Orleans, neoliberal offloading did not happen as a result of service provision. But, as we see in Chapter 4, the pressures of off-loading are ever-present in neighborhood associations, except that they are not caused by service provision, but instead by the pressure of being a watchdog for neighborhood interests across a cornucopia of governmental systems.

Neighborhood association power, as we will see, was dependent on a wide variety of factors. One of the challenges of using the neoliberalism frame in New Orleans is that it works best as a sweeping generalization. Yes, there was a "Neoliberal Deluge," as Johnson (2011a, xvii) puts it. Yes, neoliberalism is a wider category that captures so many different policies, as Adams (2013), Buras (2014), and Arena (2012) write. But it does not capture the variety that lies within the neighborhood movement. At times, neighborhood associations found themselves fighting neoliberalism directly. At other times, they found themselves supporting it. Neoliberal shifts in policy were happening all around these neighborhoods, but activists often saw things not through that ideological lens but through the lens of their own community. Rarely did neighborhood activists frame school closures as *neoliberal closures*. They posed them as *neighborhood closures*. As Chapter 3 shows, the lens was about hospitals not health care, about blight not housing policy. In short, a politics of inhabitants that focuses on urban space is geographic in nature. The primary lens of neighborhood activists is through their own neighborhood. It follows that the best way to understand their activism is to walk through the neighborhood itself.

This book does just that with fourteen neighborhoods – each with its own motives, peccadilloes, neighborhood institutions. It is not opposition to neoliberalism (or support) that motivates each association, it is neighborhood. The associations were randomly selected according to strata based on their income (see Appendix I). The sample includes geographic diversity within the city of New Orleans (though, notably, there is no association from the Lower Ninth Ward). Similarly, the neighborhoods that were selected span a wide variety of race and socio-economic categories. Data used below is from the Greater New Orleans Community Data Center's neighborhood breakdown of census data from the years 2000 and 2010 (GNOCDC), but is limited by the fact that many of the associations define their neighborhood boundaries differently than neighborhood data does.

Six associations are part of what is loosely called "Uptown New Orleans" (see Table 2.1).[1] Uptown is roughly the section to the west of the I-10 Highway, the upriver neighborhoods. It includes Audubon Park, Tulane University, and Loyola University, and is generally considered safer, wealthier, and whiter than the rest of the city, although as is seen in this sample, it includes pockets of poverty and some majority African-American neighborhoods. The six associations drawn from Uptown are the Upper Audubon Association, Fontainebleau Improvement Association, Irish Channel Neighborhood Association, Broadmoor Improvement Association, Hollygrove-Dixon Neighborhood Association, and Northwest Carrollton Neighborhood Association (though some might define Carrollton as distinct from Uptown). In the years following the storm, the Upper Audubon Association and Fontainebleau Improvement Association were almost exclusively white, with upper-class residents and high levels of home ownership. Their leaders reflected the neighborhood: the president of the Upper Audubon Association – renamed Jerry throughout this

Table 2.1 Uptown demographics

Association	Neighborhood	Population (2000)	+/- (2010)	Race (Af-Am) (2000)	+/- (2010)	Poverty (2000)	+/- (2010)
Upper Audubon Association	Audubon	14,898	+958	5.1 %	-0.3%	17.9%	+0.1%
Fontainebleau Improvement Association	Marlyville/ Fontainebleau	6,740	-991	27.9%	-4.0%	12.9%	+4.7%
Hollygrove-Dixon Neighborhood Association	Hollygrove	6,919	-2,541	94.7%	-0.7%	28.4%	-7.0%
Northwest Carrollton Neighborhood Association	Dixon	1,772	-502	94.9%	-4.6%	31.1%	+11.0%
Broadmoor Improvement Association	Broadmoor	7,232	-1,851	68.2%	-7.1%	31.8%	-17.8%
Irish Channel Neighborhood Association	Irish Channel	4,270	-897	68.4%	-28.5%	41.1%	-18.7%

book – was a white, male property owner. Twain, the president of the Fontainebleau Improvement Association, was as well. Both associations were supported by relatively younger families: Kerry and Ginny, in Fontainebleau, ran the Security Committee and Kevin, in Upper Audubon, was a New Orleans native and had recently returned to the city to buy a house for his young family. Their associations were understated and professional. The Northwest Carrollton Neighborhood Association and the Hollygrove-Dixon Neighborhood Association were located farther north and were primarily African-American. These neighborhoods were showing hints of gentrification, as poverty rates had fallen since Hurricane Katrina. The Northwest Carrollton Neighborhood Association was a tight-knit group of activists led by Jean, who ran a prominent blog, and Kristen, both middle-aged white women. The Hollygrove-Dixon Neighborhood Association was recently formed and still trying to find its feet and identify its leadership, settling on Curt, a white male who was picked to represent an African-American neighborhood despite some controversy. He was chosen primarily because of his legal experience and despite concerns about having a white male representing an overwhelmingly African-American neighborhood. The Irish Channel neighborhood made a dramatic transformation after Hurricane Katrina. Prior to the storm it had extremely high rates of poverty, but the neighborhood was one of the few in New Orleans not to flood. As a result, it gentrified, becoming whiter and wealthier. The Irish Channel Neighborhood Association reflected these changes, electing Kara, a young mother and recent home buyer in the neighborhood, to be president. The Broadmoor neighborhood has also seen a transformation, although it was largely political and happened in spite of extreme flooding. The Broadmoor Improvement Association united some of New Orleans's oldest African-American political families with middle-class residents and poor ones. The association became tremendously strong and influential, linking to members of a variety of organizations, some of whom were interviewed for this project. Jessica partnered with the Broadmoor Improvement Association to create the Apex Youth Center; Cindy was a representative on the affiliated Broadmoor Improvement District; and Bruce was a pastor at the nearby Church of Annunciation. These interviews reflected the incredible density of organizations and partnerships throughout Broadmoor in the years after the storm.

Six neighborhood associations are sampled from overwhelmingly African-American sections of the city with relatively higher levels of poverty (see Table 2.2).[2] The Historic Faubourg Lafayette Association is tucked into Central City, an area with deep ties to local politicians and African-American culture. This tiny association had its roots in a few people who had stayed in the neighborhood despite increased blight, crime, and drugs. Jennifer had run the association for over a decade after buying a home in the neighborhood, and she watched as the association eventually dissolved. Without her knowledge, a new mother (Becky) joined a long-time neighbor (Tanya) to relaunch the association. Its leadership reflected its African-American roots. Tanya, its president, was a long-time resident and African-American homeowner. Also representing the changing neighborhood was Becky, a new white mother who moved to the neighborhood because of its great location and cheap housing stock.

Gentilly is home to the Gentilly Terrace and Gardens Neighborhood Association, Dreux Avenue Good Neighbors Society, Pilotland Neighborhood Association, and Gentilly Sugar Hill Neighborhood

Table 2.2 Gentilly and New Orleans East demographics

Association	Neighborhood	Population (2000)	+/- (2010)	Race (Af-Am) (2000)	+/- (2010)	Poverty (2000)	+/- (2010)
Gentilly Terrace and Gardens Neighborhood Association	Gentilly Terrace	10,542	-2,332	69.7%	+8.1%	16.1%	+0.0%
Dreux Avenue Good Neighbors Society	Gentilly Terrace	10,542	-2,332	69.6%	+8.1%	16.1%	+0.0%
Gentilly Sugar Hill Neighborhood Association	Dillard	6,471	-2,098	88.4%	+2.9%	20.6%	-1.0%
Pilotland Neighborhood Association	St Bernard Area	6,427	-5,453	97.8%	-7.2%	66.0%	-30.7%
Historic Faubourg Lafayette Neighborhood Association	Central City	19,072	-7,815	87.1%	- 14.7%	49.8%	-11.9%
Lake Carmel Neighborhood Improvement Association	Little Woods	44,311	-12,613	86.1%	+6.5%	17.4%	+8.0%

Association. These neighborhoods were less dense than others and often complained of being forgotten amidst the more famous New Orleans neighborhoods. Gentilly is historically African-American, as it is one of the first places that African-Americans could buy property. The associations in this part of the city vary. Gentilly Terrace and Gardens Neighborhood Association had strong leadership and a history of involvement in the neighborhood. Pilotland is the opposite, a new association in a neighborhood that saw severe flooding and rapid population loss. Its neighborhood association reflects these challenges, struggling for volunteers and facing extreme challenges as a community. The final area covered by these associations is New Orleans East. This neighborhood contains the majority of the land mass in New Orleans. It is known for its subdivisions, which are typically communities of middle-class African-Americans. New Orleans East also contains much of the city's subsidized housing. The Lake Carmel

Table 2.3 French Quarter and West Bank demographics

Association	Neighborhood	Population (2000)	+/- (2010)	Race (Af-Am) (2000)	+/- (2010)	Poverty (2000)	+/- (2010)
Algiers Point Association	Algiers Point	2,381	+74	25.1%	-2.6%	17.3%	-10.8%
French Quarter Citizens Inc.	French Quarter	4,176	-363	4.3%	+0.1%	10.8%	-3.6%

community is a subdivision in the Little Woods neighborhood, and its association is indicative of a community that moved to New Orleans East to partake in a suburban version of the American dream.

The final two associations in the study are French Quarter Citizens Inc. and the Algiers Point Association (Table 2.3). The French Quarter is the most famous neighborhood in New Orleans. It attracts tourists year-round for its music, culture, architecture, and the famous and infamous Bourbon Street. Its residents are older, white, and wealthy. French Quarter Citizens Inc. represents these residents and is dedicated primarily to ensuring that tourism does not encroach upon the everyday life of residents. Algiers Point is located on the West Bank of the Mississippi River. The defining feature of the West Bank is its physical separation from the city, a separation that causes many New Orleans residents to consider the West Bank a separate city. The Algiers Point Association deals primarily with continued access to the ferry that connects the neighborhood to the French Quarter. Its members also work with law enforcement to lessen crime by individuals taking the ferry. The association is well funded; it pays a resident part-time to produce a newsletter.

Woven into the history and present of these neighborhoods are the forces of structural (Friedman 1969) and systemic racism (Feagin 2014), often manifesting through housing policies (Ladson-Billings and Tate 1995). New Orleans's own peculiar and challenging racial history provides a twist on these historical themes. Tremé, which claims the mantle of the oldest free black community in the United States, is part of a legacy of French rule that allowed for free blacks. But while there have historically been free blacks, property ownership was limited to certain neighborhoods. Neighborhoods such as Pilotland in Gentilly were among the first to allow black home ownership, and the legacy of New Orleans East was in its promise of middle-class home ownership for blacks. But such legacies are complicated, as many of the traditionally African-American neighborhoods (New Orleans East, Lower Ninth Ward) were on lower-lying land and farther from the core of the city (a notable exception is Central City). This was a result not only of active discrimination (historically, blacks were unable to buy property in more central neighborhoods) but also of forces that contributed to blacks having relatively less wealth than whites and thus being forced to live in cheaper neighborhoods that were more likely to flood. While many residents will talk of how wonderful it is to live in New Orleans close to such diverse residents, this is in part a result of the city's uneven geography. Neighborhoods with less expensive land were often packed tightly alongside wealthier neighborhoods, the primary difference being that less expensive neighborhoods were a foot or two closer to sea level and more likely to flood.

Culture works in similar ways. Traditions such as the Mardi Gras Indians evolved out of black exclusion from white Mardi Gras parades. As New Orleans's port has lost influence, these fractures have shifted again, with workers at hotels, restaurants, and bars often needing to live farther from the French Quarter, where most of the city's tourist activity takes place. The result of this racialized landscape is the foundation of the neighborhood dynamics described above.

Neighborhood associations can be both the cause of and the balm for such racial wounds. Neighborhoods are the site of organizing to ensure that residents are treated fairly. But the focus on community can turn into NIMBYism, which actively seeks to exclude people of color in the name of protecting the character of the neighborhood.

Frank, the president of the Algiers Point Association, is eloquent in describing neighborhood associations and the source of their power. In his view, power comes not from funding or from having formal roles in government processes. He tells me, "We don't actually have any formal power, but like most cities, if a neighborhood association shows up with a few people, the city listens." Frank argues that informal power is drawn from local context, a context that varies greatly. One of the primary challenges of this book is that it maps those local arguments and examples using the right to the city so that we can understand the implications of the New Orleans neighborhood movement and the ways it might manifest in other cities. The ways informal power maps onto issues of neoliberalism is the subject of Chapter 3, and the ways in which it maps onto issues of democratic and racial justice make up much of the rest of this book. For Frank and his association, informal power was about locality. He described it in terms of a conflict over the Algiers Ferry in the aftermath of Hurricane Katrina.

After the hurricane, the city and Algiers Point Association clashed over the reduction in hours for the ferry that connected Algiers Point to the French Quarter. The Algiers Ferry was not the only means for local residents to get to mainland New Orleans, but it was still the lifeblood of that neighborhood. Rather than crossing the bridge and contending with traffic and tolls, residents hopped on the ferry for free and quickly found themselves in the middle of the French Quarter with its restaurants and live music. The ferry also served as a critical function for the many service workers who lived in Algiers Point but staffed the bars, hotels, restaurants, and casinos found throughout the French Quarter.

When Crescent City Connection, the quasi-governmental nonprofit in charge of transit in the region, chose to limit the hours of the ferry after Hurricane Katrina, there was a ready-made coalition to fight the changes. There were middle-class urbanists who enjoyed the French Quarter for its cultures and service-sector workers who needed later ferry hours to get home after work. When Algiers residents asked Crescent City to extend the ferry schedule past early evening, the transit agency replied that there was no demand and considered the issue closed. Frank insisted that the ferry brought most of the folks to Algiers Point Association meetings. The issue became so all-encompassing that it threatened to engulf the entire organization. It became difficult to discuss or accomplish anything else during the meetings. So, the Algiers Point Association did what so many neighborhood groups do when a single issue becomes dominant in their neighborhood; it spun off an issue-based organization, Friends of the Ferry, to deal with the ferry so that the association could get back to business as usual.

If Frank was an officer in the battle over ferry hours, Sherry found herself in the trenches. Along with a close friend, Tracy, she ran Friends of the Ferry, made public records requests, and did all the small but time-consuming tasks that must be done between community meetings. When asked to describe her work, she said, "Out of the rage of just a few individuals, we are going to change policy." The target of that rage was Crescent City Connection, an organization created by the Louisiana State Department of Transportation to build another bridge across the Mississippi and to run the ferry. Sherry had few good things to say about Crescent City Connection, insisting that it would use any excuse to limit ferry hours or shut the ferry down completely. In response, her close friend Tracy made public records requests using her own money to photocopy what she found. Eventually, Tracy found a smoking gun – a broken promise – and that enabled Friends of the Ferry and the Algiers Point Association to leverage some power.

The political promise had been simple: the funds from the local bridge tolls would go to the ferry. For many Algiers residents, this was the silver lining to having to cross the bridge. They knew that the money they often paid for tolls helped keep the ferry free. However, an examination of Crescent City Connection's records revealed something different. Toll dollars were going towards construction on a highway, LA-1, miles to the west. Armed with this information, Friends of the Ferry went to their state representative, Pat Connic. Sherry used the information to pressure Crescent City Connection into extending the ferry hours.

This strange cocktail of volunteers and desperation was the blueprint circulated across New Orleans in the aftermath of Hurricane Katrina. Frank, Sherry, and Terry rallied around a micro-local issue, one that is difficult to map onto neoliberalism. Were they fighting neoliberalism? If neoliberalism is defined as restricting government services, then yes. Were they fighting for justice? Perhaps, particularly if one accepts the necessity of the free ferry for helping low-income workers cross into the French Quarter for work. But neoliberalism was nowhere to be found in their explanations of their fight, and the Algiers Point community that rallied around the ferry is one of the more conservative communities in New Orleans (though conservative in New Orleans has its own odd connotations, differing from much of the rest of the country). In some ways, the Algiers Ferry was participating in something fundamentally neoliberal, the neighborhood competition for scarce resources.

To call the Friends of the Ferry an organization that opposed neoliberalism is to miss the story as it is told by neighborhood activists. It is to bring an ideological and theoretical frame to a community without hearing why that community did what it did. Frank, Sherry, and Tracy were all fierce advocates of the New Orleans neighborhood movement, but they fought for the ferry for their own reasons – to protect their own neighborhood institutions and, fundamentally, to protect their own link to the historical French Quarter. That is a far cry from an anti-capitalist movement.

♦

3

Neighborhood Populism
and Broken Windows

If your playgrounds are a mess, your neighborhood is a mess.
> Jeannette, former president of the Irish
> Channel Neighborhood Association

We're about working with people ... we can't afford to be political.
> Tammy, president of the Sugar Hill
> Neighborhood Association

New Orleans had just launched its Office of Neighborhood Engagement (the name was quickly changed to Neighborhood Engagement Office to avoid confusion with Mayor Mitch Landreui's "ONE New Orleans" campaign slogan) when that office made a fundamental mistake. The office assumed that neighborhood associations would share its values and saw associations as an opportunity to address shortcomings in service delivery and to save a few precious city dollars in the process. Such an approach stands at odds with the way many theorists understand community organizations. Eldridge and Crombie (1974) argue that the best way to understand an organization is to look at its functions and its ideals. There are a host of ways to categorize nonprofits and organizations based on what they do: Blau and Scott (1962, 42) look at "who benefits" from the organization, Vickers (1972) looks at the source of financial resources, Katz and Kahn (1966) classify organizations based on what the organization does, and there are the sector definitions, such as public, private or for profit, and not for profit, that we are familiar with (Anheier and Salamon 2006). Following in these traditions, I moved away from the assumption that neighborhood associations wanted to provide social services and instead asked them what was important and what they did.

The results are important for the wider discussion of neoliberalism, justice, and neighborhood movements. The ideals of neighborhood associations split along neighborhood lines, with the majority of associations seeking to "protect" their neighborhood, while a minority focus on "neighborhood change." The logic and coalition underlying these categories do not map well onto neoliberalism or justice debates. For some, protection means protecting home values. For others, protection means addressing blight that radically alters the lived experience of those most vulnerable, largely low-income homeowners unfortunate enough to live next to a blighted property. An issue as simple as blight – critical in the years after Hurricane Katrina when the housing stock was damaged – can reinforce neoliberal logic or contradict it. For some homeowners, their primary motivation is the protection of an investment made in their house. For others, there is a justice motivation. Blight walks point out the injustices in a neighborhood where those with fewer resources are more likely to be "stuck" on a block next to a blighted house. For these unfortunate homeowners without the capital to move elsewhere, the problems of a blighted home become the problems of their own. The rodent problems that develop in a blighted house extend to *their* house. Flooding from the open windows and doors of a blighted house causes flood damage to shared walls. The problems of squatters and drug use in a blighted home become theirs because safety risks and concerns move to the house next door.

These neighborhood ideals of protection and change are just that: they are neighborhood focused. But far from lining up with an anti- (or pro-) neoliberalism ideology, they manifest something I call here *new urban populism* (see Edsall 2013; Blumgart 2013). New urban populism focuses on local institutions and largely sits outside the right/left ideological spectrum, although it often aligns itself with progressive politicians and politics.[1] Neighborhood associations, starting with what Leontidou (2010) calls *parochial* interests, have built from the *micro-local* level to achieve a coherent political philosophy that prioritizes institutions, buildings, and stability while building a coalition across individuals that would likely be opposed politically or ideologically.

The Algiers Point Association demonstrates what this neighborhood protection model looks like and how it can cut both ways, for and against neoliberalism. Yes, the Algiers Point Association fought to keep its ferry to the French Quarter open. But that was riding a wave, an issue that emerged after the storm and brought a huge influx of residents to association meetings. Yet the association president, Frank, describes the daily duties of the presidency quite differently. He has been mostly concerned with dealing with crime in the neighborhood. These responsibilities, one to protect a neighborhood institution and the second to address criminal activity, get to the heart of what neighborhood activists in New Orleans called the "crime and blight association." And Frank performed his role within that system well. He had a good relationship with the police and the cellphone of a ranking officer so that he could go directly to the top of the chain when necessary. But Algiers Point Association members talk about crime moved quickly to the darker sides of neighborhood protectionism. Frank worried about corrupt police and even mentioned busting a prostitution ring in the neighborhood. Neighbors fear that the neighborhood is at risk of crime sprees with criminals taking the ferry into their neighborhood. Rumors of such criminal activity circulate periodically in the community.

The role of a neighborhood association here is one of enabling. In a political climate such as post-Katrina New Orleans, the demand for political participation in response to insider/outsider critiques of local politics is tremendous; this role is one of the fundamental functions of local politics and a way to stem the criticism that outsiders are privileged over residents. But these policies depend upon someone actually doing the participating, and those who participate are rarely doing so because participation is such a beautiful thing; rather, they are driven by specific local concerns. Sometimes that motivation is fear. Nowhere is this truer than in community policing. The demand for community policing, in which cops walk their beats, have relationships with community members, and listen to the community, is almost universal. Walk into a community meeting anywhere in urban United States and you hear about walking beats. Police officers attend neighborhood association meetings and urge residents to call anonymous tip lines if they see or hear anything suspicious. The same is true in New Orleans, where the police not only go to association meetings, but hold their own New Orleans Neighbors and Police Anti-Crime Council (better known as NONPACC) meetings. Of course, these meetings assume someone shows up, just as building relationships in the community assumes a second person with whom to build a relationship. In New Orleans, the role of *just showing up* often fell to neighborhood associations. The idea of attending an endless barrage of planning meetings, police meetings, neighborhood meetings, and others was too much for any individual, so the association stepped in to make sure seats were filled. When "participation" or "community policing" happens in New Orleans, neighborhood associations are often the silent partner. And that comes with challenges. Nationally, the #BlackLivesMatter movement has highlighted issues of police brutality within communities as well as wider systemic issues, including *broken windows policing*, whose strict enforcement falls disproportionately on black and brown bodies. Community policing can amplify those distortions because reporting suspicious activity depends upon the eye of the volunteering beholder. With an increasing research base that shows unconscious bias in the way people of color are viewed (Greenwald and Krieger 2006), there is a risk of conflating danger and discrimination.

This struggle is at the center of the neighborhood association model. Over and over again, neighborhood associations built neighborhood protection writ large and security writ small. Eight of the fourteen associations in this sample defined crime as among their highest priorities. Of the six that did not, five of them identified other aspects that loosely fall under the broader theme of neighborhood protectionism, such as preservation, blight, and quality of life. This focus on crime manifested itself through a variety of tools that brought greater security to the community. Some associations, such as the Irish Channel Neighborhood Association, started a neighborhood watch program to be run by the association. Others, such as the Algiers Point Association, coordinated closely with a neighborhood watch already active in their neighborhood. The Fontainebleau Improvement Association launched a spin-off organization that hired off-duty police officers to patrol the neighborhood.[2] Other neighborhood associations went even further, using state legislation to create a tax district to fund private security. That was the path for the Lake Carmel Improvement Association in New Orleans East and the Upper Audubon Association in Uptown.

These associations are quite diverse. Some, such as those in Fontainebleau and Upper Audubon, are in upscale neighborhoods. Others, such as Lake Carmel Improvement Association, is a neighborhood in New Orleans East, where African-Americans were promised an opportunity to pursue a middle-class dream of home ownership.

The Irish Channel is a rapidly changing neighborhood that had struggled with disinvestment before Hurricane Katrina, but saw rapid changes afterwards because it did not flood during the storm. The common link across these associations was that they saw crime as a primary challenge to the success of a neighborhood, and for some, the success of their investment as homeowners.

The neighborhood protection ideal is not solely the motive behind increased security programs. It also serves as motivation for addressing blight – a critical issue across New Orleans after Hurricane Katrina when so many houses were damaged. The logic behind addressing blight was simple. Mary, a former activist with the Irish Channel Neighborhood Association, said it best: "Nobody is going to buy a house next to a blighted house, and nobody is going to buy a house where they don't feel safe."

Her neighborhood, the Irish Channel, faced the challenges of redlining and disinvestment after the oil crash of the 1980s. Mary and Jeannette, partners in crime and leaders of the association, spent years in the neighborhood at a time when "the neighborhood was dangerous then and the housing stock beat up." Jeannette often found herself on the front lines, with criminal activity all around her. Quite the storyteller, she describes being on a first-name basis with what she called the "drug boys." She told them, "You don't sell drugs on your momma's [sic] porch, don't sell them on mine." As she tells it, when a local delivery-man was selling drugs on his route, Jeannette tried to get the company to fire him. After months of no response, she finally saw a cop pull up alongside the delivery truck. But much to her dismay, the cop was buying drugs, not catching the delivery-man. So, Jeannette started writing daily postcards to the company. Along the way, the postman read them, the folks at the local post office read them, and the secretaries at the company read them. Pretty soon, everyone knew about the drug sales, and the company was forced to reassign the delivery-man to another community.

Even before Katrina, Jeannette was a firm believer in the work of "crime and blight" associations. She worried that homes would be abandoned and demolished in the neighborhood, resulting in the loss of its historical character. The historical housing was one of the few assets in the neighborhood. To stop the demolitions, she applied for, and received, a historical designation for the neighborhood. She prepared the application by making a photocopy of a successful application from the city, and then cutting and pasting a hard copy into a new application to ensure that her application would be successful.

In some neighborhoods, the focus on blight led to different strategies. In Algiers Point, Faubourg Lafayette, Pilotland, and Hollygrove-Dixon, the associations focused on cataloguing blighted properties to get the city to do something about owners who left their properties as they were after the storm. Throughout the city, neighborhoods held blight walks, a way of combining politicians' needs for photo-ops with the neighborhood's desire to highlight individual properties that were both dangerous and bad investments. The tools for doing this were contentious. As seen in Chapter 6, the demolition of blighted homes became a critical issue not just in regard to preservation, but because of governmental corruption. Code enforcement, in which the city levied fines for not keeping a property inhabitable, was similarly controversial. Some neighborhood associations loved such enforcement and actively participated in the prosecution of absent owners – to such an extent that the city held a multi-day training program on how to submit evidence at code enforcement hearings without having to take a day off work. But these hearings could also be extremely hard on low-income homeowners struggling to get back to the city. The city, and neighborhood associations, labored to find the balance between being lenient with homeowners and cracking down on investors who caused damage to neighborhoods by letting properties sit. Neighborhood associations often played a critical role in such deliberations, with their testimony for (or against) a property owner serving as a type of unofficial tie-breaker in code enforcement hearings.

Other neighborhoods focused on making their communities more attractive not solely through enforcement, but through improving the infrastructure in their neighborhood. One particularly popular approach was to plant neighborhood trees. With so many trees uprooted or killed during the storm, tree-planting nonprofits thrived – they fit the perfect niche in both improving a neighborhood's aesthetics and tying them to the historical nature of New Orleans's neighborhoods, which had long prided themselves for the historical oak trees lining neighborhood boulevards. For associations such as the Northwest Carrollton Neighborhood Association where much of the association activity focused on contentious development, working with one of those nonprofits was like taking a breath of fresh air. For Northwest Carrollton Neighborhood Association President Kristen, Hike 4 Katreena was important because "we were both doing it from the heart." This contrasted with so many of her neighborhood activities, which were power struggles. Hike 4 Katreena and a similar nonprofit called Parkway worked with a host of neighborhood associations, including the Fontainebleau Improvement Association, Sugar Hill Neighborhood Association, the Irish Channel Neighborhood Association, and Gentilly Terrace and Gardens Neighborhood Association. These nonprofits built their post-Katrina clientele in New Orleans by finding willing partners and taking advantage of neighborhoods' eagerness to improve their physical surroundings. While these tree-planting partnerships were big-ticket items within associations – they could point to new trees, and often it was a big event, requiring lots of volunteers to plant the trees in a single day – neighborhood associations did a million little things on a weekly, monthly, or annual basis to improve the physical nature of their neighborhoods. The Fontainebleau Improvement Association paid to have their trees sprayed for caterpillars each year. Virtually every association held clean-up days, and the more ambitious associations, such as the Broadmoor Improvement Association, converted post-Katrina volunteers from across the country into neighborhood beautification workers.

These different concerns of neighborhood associations – crime, blight and code enforcement, and neighborhood beautification – closely mirror aspects of broken windows theory that have developed over the decades since the theory's introduction into the public lexicon by Wilson and Kelling's (1982) famous *Atlantic* article. This article highlights Zimbardo's (1969) research, in which he placed an abandoned car in a middle-class neighborhood and a second car in a low-income neighborhood. In the low-income neighborhood, the car was stripped almost immediately. In the middle-class neighborhood, it sat for weeks, until Zimbardo smashed the windshield. Only then was it stripped. The implication is that the physical condition of neighborhoods sends small messages to those within about the ability to commit crime and get away with it.

For years, broken windows theory has translated into an argument for strict enforcement of petty crimes, an idea popularized by Mayor Rudy Giuliani's success in New York City and in the public consciousness by Malcolm Gladwell's telling of how New York limited illegal riding of public transit by publicly and visibly rounding up violators (2000). Gladwell argues that similar broken windows strategies – designed to send a signal by limiting small violations – helped decrease crime, although this assertion is now contested, as Giuliani's "success" mirrored lower crime rates across the country that occurred without the use of these strategies. The popularity of broken windows theory supported crime-stopping initiatives such as stop-and-frisk and other public policies designed to catch and punish every crime.

The focus on security in these neighborhood associations bears similarities to the crime focus of broken windows theory. Perhaps more officers, or more security, or more eyes, reporting simple crimes or even suspicious activity, could limit criminal activity (though recent research has soured on these strategies). The focus on blight enforcement harkens back to the original metaphor – that it is the broken windows themselves that encourage crime. Thus, perhaps instead of eliminating vandals who throw rocks at broken windows, neighborhoods should ensure that the windows themselves are fixed. And finally, associations repurpose broken windows theory into what one neighborhood activist in Camden, NJ, calls "Flower Box Development," in which, instead of focusing on eliminating negative images in a neighborhood to reduce crime (and improve property values), neighborhood leaders should focus on adding visually appealing aspects to their neighborhood.

A rare few associations explicitly reject this crime and blight model. Sometimes that process plays out as a conflict and power struggle within an association. In the Irish Channel, the neighborhood association functioned for decades as a crime- and blight-focused institution. But after the storm a younger group of parents moved to the neighborhood. These new parents saw the crime and blight model as punitive and anti-youth. Instead of adding security to their neighborhood, they wanted to add opportunities for young people. The Rachel Simms Baptist Ministry had historically run youth sports programs in the nearby Lyons-Burke Park, but after damage to their offices during Hurricane Katrina, the ministry closed shop. That left two distinct problems in the community: the first was a gap in youth services, the second was a now-vacant park that once had been a vibrant neighborhood center. Shifting the focus to youth services made sense.

Anna, a young mother and relatively new resident of the neighborhood, joined a couple of similarly minded individuals to run a slate of candidates for the neighborhood association's board. They won the election and immediately turned their focus to finding a partner for youth programming. The natural fit was the New Orleans Recreation Department (NORD). NORD provided youth programs in which the department provided a league and structure if a partnering organization could create a "booster club" that fundraised and supplied coaches. While normally NORD worked with community centers or other small nonprofits, the Irish Channel Neighborhood Association adapted the model for neighborhood associations and launched the Lyons-Burke Booster Club. The result was baseball and basketball leagues in the park.

The Broadmoor association took a similar path. From the beginning, it worked with Annunciation Church. The church was a co-writer of grants, built a campus to house volunteers, and was an extremely close partner. Bruce, the executive director of the Annunciation mission, had a motto: "It's really hard for people to hear the gospel if their stomach is rumbling too hard." That motto was central to Broadmoor; the association focused on helping residents rather than catching miscreants. The strategy of support, not enforcement, in turn, attracted other institutions and volunteers. Cindy, who volunteered for the association and put together maps of who had returned to the neighborhood, insisted: "We are about prevention and proactive governance, not about [sic] punitive." That attitude also attracted Jessica. Her dream was to start a community center for youth. She had gone to several neighborhoods, but associations were not supportive. They were worried that such a center would bring the wrong kids to their neighborhood and prove more trouble than it was worth. But Broadmoor welcomed her with open arms. Her Apex Youth Center became part of the neighborhood's education corridor alongside a local library and charter school. When Broadmoor realized that tax districts, which neighborhood associations were promoting to finance private security, could be used only for "punitive" purposes, they went to the state to lobby for new legislation. That legislation allowed for the creation of the Broadmoor Improvement District, a tax district that gave wide discretion to the Broadmoor Improvement Association to use the funds to improve the neighborhood, not just security. When the Broadmoor Improvement District's board was elected, both Cindy and Jennifer filled slots. On the board, they were empowered to use tax dollars to implement the values that encouraged them to volunteer with the association in the first place.

During my time in the city, the Gentilly Terrace and Gardens Association showed signs of a similar transformation in progress. There, a young pastor started a church called Nola Church Plant. He used that church as an opportunity to increase programming for youth in the neighborhood. As he became more involved with the association, he tried to push it in the same direction.

While the "crime and blight" associations dominate the New Orleans landscape, there is a movement towards more progressive associations that reject the punitive aspects of the crime and blight model. These associations most often involve young, idealistic volunteers with young children and a partnership, in some way, with a faith-based institution (and an affiliated faith-based value set). That should not be a surprise. Faith-based institutions themselves have long provided secular social services in urban communities (Cnaan 2006). They too have proved capable of influencing neighborhood associations to do the same.

Although neighborhood associations differ in their attitudes towards punitive crime and blight models, they share a common commitment to the institutions in their neighborhoods. In virtually every neighborhood, organization swirled around ensuring that local infrastructure and local institutions are maintained. In Algiers Point, the association's primary geographical feature was the way the Mississippi River separated the neighborhood from mainland New Orleans. Consequently, its dominant issue was its ferry.

In the Irish Channel, new volunteers to the association filled vacant parks with youth programs.

In the Broadmoor, the neighborhood was at risk of losing both its library and public school. It raised millions of dollars for the library and actively recruited a charter school to the neighborhood.

In Hollygrove-Dixon, the association focused on its public school. Its president proudly recounted the story of the city's superintendent calling the school to inquire about possible cheating. Apparently the district was surprised by high standardized test scores. The association focused on fundraisers for the school.

In the Fontainebleau Improvement Association and the Northwest Carrollton Neighborhood Association, the foci were key plots of land that could potentially attract a business. In Fountainebleau, neighbors proactively sought a grocery store for the neighborhood. In Northwest Carrollton, residents fought against a layout and design that meant that the back of a Walgreens, with almost two dozen dumpsters, would face their community.

The same was true across the city, as protests focused on the reopening of Charity Hospital (Lovell 2011) and public housing projects (Arena 2013). These protests were not against broad public policies, but about specific, local institutions that affected the daily lives of residents.

In some neighborhoods, this interest in maintaining neighborhood institutions takes the form of preservation. The Irish Channel and the Historic Faubourg Lafayette Association both created historical districts in response to the demolition or abandonment (and consequent looting) of historical homes after the oil crises of the 1980s. In Faubourg Lafayette, neighborhood leaders developed a system to track the black market for accessories from historical houses. Sitting on a porch, Jennifer, the former president of the association, told me that to this day she did not polish her historical brass door handle because someone would walk off with it. At the time, she claimed, there was a thriving black market and banks would often illegally buy items from soon-to-be demolished homes. The neighborhood association suspected the involvement of local banks, but the banks firmly denied it. So the association set up an alarm system: if someone saw an individual stealing from abandoned homes, they would follow the individual (who often would be pushing a grocery cart full of house accessories) all the way to the bank. Once, according to Jennifer, the bank denied involvement in trade even with the grocery cart still in full view. For Historic Faubourg Lafayette and the Irish Channel, creating a historical district was a way to protect housing stock from looting. In the French Quarter, the pressure comes not from looting, but from the repurposing of land from residential use to commercial use. French Quarter Citizens Inc. and the Vieux Carré Property Owners, Residents, and Associates both see the growth of tourism as a threat to their residential way of life and view the preservation movement as a way to oppose such growth.

The arc of this second preservation critique parallels what Harvey (2012) calls the Disneyfication of urban cores. In New Orleans, the comparison I heard more often was to Williamsburg, VA. In Colonial Williamsburg, people no longer live the lifestyle that draws tourists. The town is, in effect, a museum or an artifact. Residents worry that the same thing will happen to New Orleans. Over time, concessions in attempts to draw tourists to the French Quarter will overwhelm the residential experience. Residents will leave as it becomes more and more difficult to lead a normal life, tipping the balance of interests towards tourists while simultaneously undermining the living culture that tourists come to see. This is the heart of Disneyfication: a real neighborhood has been converted into a theme park, and with this done the living aspects of the culture disappear within the city and leave it as nothing more than a tourist attraction.

This struggle plays out in almost every issue that French Quarters Inc. and the Vieux Carré Property Owners, Residents, and Associates address. Historical preservation is key to ensuring that new properties still fit in and contribute to the neighborhood. Preservation and architecture are used to oppose development that would overrun residential properties and transform neighborhoods in ways that detract from the quality of life for those who live there. In many ways, this is a key manifestation of the right to the city; it is a counterbalance to what one French Quarter preservationist calls "developer's logic." *Developer's logic* uses short-term economic arguments – typically, jobs produced and trickle-down effects to surrounding businesses – to make the case for development, even if that development does not fit the character of the neighborhood or might ultimately undermine the long-term economics of the neighborhood. Because developer's logic so often compares a single development to no development at all, the logic of "jobs and economic impact" always supports the argument that development should occur. Activists in the French Quarter often find themselves fighting this logic. Some use the "character of the neighborhood" as a case. Others make more technocratic arguments, claiming that there should not be exceptions to zoning and the master plan in the city. Many neighborhood associations make the case that neighborhoods should prioritize their residents *beyond* development. This last case is deeply embedded in the logic of the right to the city, which, at a basic level, is about the right to use urban space in ways that benefit residents (Leontidou 2010). Purcell (2002) even argues that the right to the city is unique in its creation of a residential *right* to influence development. At the core of the New Orleans neighborhood movement is a related idea – that informal neighborhood organizing should be able to push back against developers that have political and practical power.

This sets up fundamental questions. What do neighborhood associations do with this power? How should we interpret the results of such involvement in development? Most critically, the involvement of neighborhoods in development sets up critical questions about NIMBYism, for NIMBYism is everywhere in this discussion. In the French Quarter, hotels are opposed because they surpass height limits. Short-term rentals like the popular AirBnB are opposed because they restrict long-term renting and flood residential communities with tourists. At the corner of Bourbon and Canal, a brass band was reported for playing late into the night. Local activists lobby for enforcement of noise codes for bars blasting music. In the Marigny, Mimi's, a neighborhood bar that built a reputation after the storm for great live music, was temporarily shut down because it did not have a live music license.

These NIMBY struggles, discussed further in Chapter 5, also point out a simplifying assumption that underpins much study of community. Communities are not universal entities, and empowering them can actually divide them. Empowerment pits a class of homeowners who have long made money renting out their homes during Mardi Gras and Jazz Fest against residential activists who deal with purchasers who buy residential homes solely for the purpose of short-term rentals and the never-ending battery of bachelor parties that populate the neighborhood with that purchase. In the fourteen neighborhoods in this sample, twice there were major neighborhood conflicts over proposed grocery stores – presumably the least controversial development possible. *Everyone* wants high-quality grocery stores in urban neighborhoods. But placing neighborhood activists in the middle of development decisions can pit preservationists against communities in need of jobs or those seeking to protect residential life against those seeking to protect New Orleans's cultural heritage.

This neighborhood ideology, one that prioritizes crime and blight that builds around neighborhood institutions and seeks to protect and preserve neighborhood buildings and cultures, is important to right to the city arguments about development and to the neighborhood movement after Hurricane Katrina. It is, as Leontindou (2010, 1190) calls it, "parochial." It is specific to the neighborhood context and, as such, is less an urban social movement and more a parallel ideology that plays out uniquely in each and every community, often in conflicting ways in a given neighborhood. But it also plays out politically. This parochial, micro-local politics is the manifestation of what Purcell (2008) identifies in *Recapturing Democracy*. It is the neighborhood politics that he thinks is a counterbalance for neoliberalism. Yet, this neighborhood ideology is not grounded in neoliberalism or its opposition. At times it opposes neoliberal development as it did Disneyfication in the French Quarter, but at times it reinforces neoliberalism by building a crime and blight infrastructure designed to maximize property values and, potentially, exclude lower-income individuals from owning homes. At its ugliest, this neighborhood ideology embraces the worst of NIMBYism, excluding the less fortunate through both price and opposition to services for the homeless or for returning felons. Neighborhood populism is not fundamentally about neoliberalism, it is a form of populism that manifests itself as politically agnostic, not emphasizing a left-leaning or right-leaning politics, but rather a priority of the local over both left-leaning and right-leaning politics, although, as Edsall (2013) and Blumgart (2013) point out, the governing coalitions that collaborate with such a movement are often quite progressive.

This neighborhood populism is best understood walking through a neighborhood; there anyone can see the local institutions and quality of life issues that motivate neighborhood populists. To understand that, let us leave New Orleans and examine the origins of urban populism in Cleveland, where the concept of urban populism was popularized by Dennis Kucinich (Swanstrom 1985), another politician who blended progressivism with this ideologically agnostic focus on local institutions. Kucinich's populism centered around two key issues faced by the city of Cleveland in the late 1970s. The first issue was corporate subsidies, and the second was the potential sale of the city-owned power utility Muni Light. Swanstrom (ibid.) largely focuses on the populist roots of opposing sweetheart deals for downtown corporations, which did not have to pay taxes. He links opposition to these deals to a desire to give tax breaks directly to citizens, long a populist issue both inside and outside urban areas. But once Kucinich was mayor, he set aside these low income tax populist tendencies for a different brand of populism. He fought desperately to keep the ownership of Muni Light with the city, even tying it to a tax increase, both of which overwhelmingly passed in a referendum. When Kucinich lost to Republican George Voinivich in his next election, it was in part because Voinivich had mimicked his stance on Muni Light by refusing to sell the public utility.

In that early struggle with the first popularized urban populist, we can see the seeds of a neighborhood ideology that prioritizes local institutions over partisan politics – the same ideology found not just in New Orleans's neighborhood but also in Newark, Camden, and New York City. Just as Kucinich rode a wave of support for a public institution (Muni Light), progressive mayors such as Ras Baraka of Newark and Bill De Blasio of New York have ridden waves of support for traditional public schools and against closing them for charters and other options to complement their progressive base. In Camden, New Jersey, Governor Chris Christie and Mayor Dana Redd replaced the city-run police force with a county force. Residents embraced new urban populism, rising up and signing close to three thousand petitions for a referendum, a massive number in a city where approximately five thousand votes can win a mayoral election (though they ultimately lost this effort in court). Each of these examples shows a fierce protectionism and pride in local institutions alongside skepticism of outside control. Residents in both Cleveland and Camden did not see their cities as blank slates; they were responding to threats to their institutions and neighborhoods. In New York, Mayor Bloomberg talked of using cities as policy experiments (Barbaro 2013). The specter of being used as an experiment hung heavily over New Orleans after the storm. Most famously, the school system was dramatically altered as traditional public schools were closed and charter schools opened, something Berkshire (2014, n.p.) satirically called "America's urban education laboratory." A similar shift happened in health care, where care for low-income residents was shifted from Charity Hospital to health clinics (see DeSalvo 2010). Those clinics eventually lost their funding (Rittenhouse et al. 2012). The same is true of public housing: the Department of Housing and Urban Development used the storm as pretense to evacuate and demolish the Lafitte Project and shift it to a less dense model. Each of these reforms came with little democratic input. Roberta Gratz (2015) sums up local feeling towards using the city for experiments in the title of her book, *We're Still Here Ya Bastards*. Residents do not want to be the subject of experiments. This neighborhood ideology is an embrace of long-standing local institutions over change without democratic control.

Those arguing that Newark and New York are part of a new urban populism (Edsall 2013; Blumgart 2013), moving cities to the left, are correct, but they ignore a key aspect of that populism: communities are being activated not primarily by progressive values, but by risks to institutions in their own communities. Whether it be the dissolution of a police force in Camden, of public schools in Newark and New York, or of a municipal utility authority in Cleveland, the traditional progressive coalition is strengthened by residents voting on a micro-local axis. By focusing on institutions and local conditions, local activists extricate themselves from partisanship in the traditional sense.

Kucinich is, again, a critical example of the manner in which urban populism can transcend, or simply ignore, partisanship. Swanstrom (1985) notes that Kucinich's rise happened largely outside of the Democratic Party, despite his being a Democrat. He had few contacts within the establishment and essentially ran against it. His views, built upon supporting local institutions, not large corporations, departed widely from Democratic and Republican consensus. Something similar is starting to happen in the education sector, where progressives concerned with social justice, urban minorities concerned with their institutions, and even tea-party Republicans concerned with government control are binding together to oppose education policies. And, in the New Orleans's battles over public housing and development, more strange bedfellows emerged. Often, the political coalitions that opposed massive development projects or the demolition of public housing were a mix of local community members who feared loss in their neighborhoods, the preservation movement that cared for the structures being eliminated, and those in surrounding communities who feared gentrification. These coalitions are examples of politics that exist away from the partisan dichotomy. With congressional approval dismal for both parties, neighborhood populism is an alternative. It is a form of micro-local politics that focuses so much on the local pothole and the local school that it can disengage from high-level, party-driven, political gridlock. For politicians such as Kucinich, Ras Baraka, and Bill De Blasio it can be a way to harness public support for local institutions and ride that wave of support to office.

It may prove that future movements serve primarily to support progressive movements naturally, as happened in the cases of Newark and New York. But, in New Orleans, neighborhood populism did not always play out that way. This sort of populism underpins many actions in New Orleans and is a unifying theme across issues that may seem politically opposed. For example, the Hollygrove-Dixon Neighborhood Association and the Broadmoor Improvement Association find themselves on radically different ends of the educational policy spectrum. One supports a neighborhood school, the other a charter school. But the unifying factor between them is support for local institutions that they view as critical to their neighborhood.

In Hollygrove-Dixon, Curt needed a unifying strategy to rally his young neighborhood association. As a relatively affluent white man, he stood out from his mostly black neighbors. He was asked to become president by the association's leadership, even while hearing grumbling about his race from the rank-and-file membership. Curt chose to build upon local institutions, particularly the neighborhood's local school, the Mary McLeod Bethune Elementary School of Literature and Technology. Curt's largest event while president was a fundraiser for the school, to which he brought Grammy award-winning singer and Bethune alum Irma Thomas back to the neighborhood. That event clearly built on these themes of local institutions and helped the floundering neighborhood association widen its base.

In Broadmoor, the association took a different approach. It recruited the Andrew H. Wilson Charter School to open in a vacant neighborhood school building. The association remained closely linked to the school, even ensuring that the school board included neighborhood parents and activists.

When these two neighborhoods are viewed from the perspective of the broader education reform movement, which often pits charters against traditional public schools, or from that of neoliberal critiques (see Buras 2014) that see school reform as a vestige of neoliberalism, they appear to represent opposite strategies. Indeed, in Hollygrove-Dixon the urban legend is that after test scores came in, Paul Pastorek, the school district's superintendent, called the school because he was so surprised that the high scores could come from a traditional public school. Curt's neighborhood association looks to the education policy maven like a firm traditionalist opposing a neoliberal school takeover. That same education policy maven would look at the Broadmoor Improvement Association and see an education reform advocate; the association specifically recruited a charter school.

But that gap disappears in conversations with residents and association members. Jenny, a board member of the Broadmoor Improvement Association, made it perfectly clear that the school was the centerpiece of the neighborhood: "You need a school in your neighborhood. It's an anchor that keeps people there." She explained that many other neighborhoods had history, or tourist attractions, or something else to draw people, but that Broadmoor needed to depend on institutions such as schools and libraries because "it's just part of the utopian thing. Everyone wants a great school." Curt made a similar argument, that a struggling association with limited volunteers needed to start with its institutions. These neighborhood leaders prioritized local needs over city-wide policy and, in doing so, provided an alternative to partisan struggles.

Those examples, like much of the support for ferries, hospitals, and other critical local institutions, do not map well onto the neoliberal debate or Purcell's (2008) assertion that democracy can serve as a counterbalance to neoliberalism. They show instead a neighborhood populism that puts aside partisanship and instead starts from the micro-local. Yes, neighborhood associations work at times to support neoliberalism and at times to oppose it, but they always work to strengthen their own local institutions. Their neighborhood populism comes first.

◆

4

Hiding behind Letterhead

Great leaders would emerge, then burn out or move on.
>   Frank, president of the Algiers Point Association

I'm new at being president; they threw me under the bus with that.
>   Tanya, president of the Faubourg Lafayette Association

The New Orleans neighborhood movement is premised on the idea of reorganizing local democracy around geographically based organizations. But Purcell (2006, 1922) challenges this idea, arguing that assuming more local scales of governance are necessarily more democratic is to fall into the "local trap." Instead, moving governance to local scales may reinforce injustices and inequities. To further complicate matters, governance itself is shifting from clearly delineating responsibilities emanating from government to a network of informal actors (Kooiman 1993). Sørenson and Torfing (2003, 196) argue that "governance networks might contribute to an efficient governance of our complex and functionally differentiated societies, but the question is whether governance networks also lead to democratic governance." This concept of democratic justice is highly debated. Is moving to a networked model either complementary or incompatible with democratic values? In other words, are these informal systems enabling backroom deals with elites suffering "from the absence of open competition, legitimacy problems, and the lack of transparency, publicity and accountability" (Sørensen and Torfing 2005, 200)? Or are they mediating institutions providing critical bridges to a government grown too technocratic to relate to the community it represents (Berger and Neuhaus 1977; Boyte 1980)? The wider debate about the New Orleans neighborhood movement asks whether a movement premised on increasing democratic links to community is itself democratic.

This debate is a daily reality in neighborhood associations, which claim to represent urban neighborhoods and participate in "invited spaces" (Lowndes and Sullivan 2008) within government as such a representative. But are they democratic?

Davis (1990) calls homeowner's associations neighborhood fascism. An employee at a local housing nonprofit said the same thing to me about neighborhood associations. After the storm, her position was to work with neighborhood associations and their demands. A city council staffer put it differently: "Without them coming to us, we wouldn't know there was an issue," but that, at the same time, some associations were clearly little more than a couple of volunteers hiding behind letterhead. Wendall Pierce, a local actor who has starred in both *Tremé* and *The Wire*, put it more sharply, accusing the Faubourg Marigny Improvement Association of being "a front for developers posing as civic activists to dominate and control the real estate for profit" (Cunningham 2015, n.p.).

That idea, that a few people use neighborhood associations as a political tool to claim the voice of the entire neighborhood, goes to the heart of democratic critiques of neighborhood organizing and distinguishes it from social movements that use participatory democracy (see Polletta 2002). Does focusing on small, urban geographic units actually disempower people? Does moving to informal systems that assume participation actually just allow those with more connections or the loudest voices to work the system more effectively? Is there a "tyranny of structurelessness" (Freeman 1972, 151) within neighborhood movements?

On the surface, neighborhood associations have the democratic infrastructure to prevent these abuses. According to the neighborhood association census I conducted with City-Works, associations have remarkable representative democratic infrastructures. Eighty-six per cent of associations hold neighborhood elections to choose their leaders. Seventy-seven per cent use parliamentary procedure, chiefly Robert's Rules of Order. Eighty-five per cent have bylaws or a constitution. These are structural signs that neighborhood associations run themselves as democratic institutions – they embrace elections, bylaws, and parliamentary procedure. On the surface, they appear to be democratic, and infrastructure for a traditionally democratic organization exists. But neighborhood associations are rarely so straightforward, a finding that echoes Polletta's (2002, 194) argument that "formal rules and ideological commitments are not enough to explain how a deliberative process actually operates." In most neighborhood association

elections, candidates run unopposed. When leaders from these associations tell their stories, they uniformly assert that finding volunteers to
run for offices posed their greatest challenge, and associations bend
over backwards to attract volunteers. It was a process I experienced
up close at a Coliseum Square Neighborhood Association meeting.

Coliseum Square is a tiny neighborhood tucked into the well-
to-do Garden District. It was an unlikely place for one's first lesson
about neighborhood democracy: volunteers are scarce, and volunteers – not votes – drive neighborhood activism. The Coliseum Square
Neighborhood Association was founded in 1972. By the time
Hurricane Katrina hit, it had fought its most important battle, the
attempt to demolish the nearby C.J. Peete public housing project
(Arena 2012) and keep scatter-site low-income housing out of the
neighborhood.[1] That battle having passed, the neighborhood association had turned to less hot-button issues, such as provision of bags
to people walking their dogs in a local park.

With less-controversial issues came fewer volunteers. Just a handful
of folks attended the annual meeting to elect officers on meeting on
June 22, 2010. Fewer than a dozen people, including this author as
an observer, sat around a single table in a local restaurant for the
meeting. As the outgoing president slowly worked his way through
the nominations for the association's elected board, the table quietly
realized that no one had been nominated for vice-president. Jokingly,
one resident nominated me. Or, I thought it was a joke. The rationales
followed fast and furious: you seem intelligent; you care about the
neighborhood; it would only be until we can find someone else.

I politely declined, but the lesson stuck. In other associations, the
crux of neighborhood association elections was not the votes, it was
who volunteered to run in the first place. These neighborhood associations claimed to represent their communities, but they did so
through a democratic process limited by the lack of volunteers rather
than one fueled by the election cycle.

I was not the only one to experience these elections more as efforts
to avoid being elected than as attempts to fill positions. Tom, the
pastor of Nola Church Plant, a small church that had just moved into
the Gentilly Terrace and Gardens neighborhood, had his own war
story from that association's latest election. Upon his move to the
neighborhood, he got involved with the association, but mostly to
encourage it to consider a new purpose. He argued that "the agenda
is driven by who shows up" and that the association focused on crime

and blight. Tom had what he called a "different agenda." He wanted to focus on relationships and serving the needs of the community and youth.[2] That agenda faced opposition, but as elections neared, another dynamic operated. Tom called those elections "battles of attrition," arguing that the president was elected because "she didn't say 'no' loud enough." In fact, despite his differing vision, they asked him to be president, even though he had only attended one or two meetings. He refused, claiming he had neither the credibility in the community nor the patience to take the position. But that did not stop him from pushing his agenda. He used his church and its volunteers to propose and co-sponsor events for youth and African-American families jointly with the association. At most Gentilly Terrace and Gardens Neighborhood Association meetings, attendees were primarily white, elderly, and middle class. At a co-sponsored outdoor showing of *The Lion King* in the park, the demographics flipped. The event drew more minorities, more children, and featured fewer Robert's Rules of Order. The park had been refurbished and featured creative, movable foam pieces. Tom's parishioners volunteered to clean up afterwards. The event was lively, entertaining, and clearly a success. It was one of a series of summer activities that Nola Church Plant co-sponsored with the association that summer, to go along with Tom's attempts to bring youth into the park on a daily basis.

Tom's first experience – the leadership's difficulty recruiting volunteers – was common across neighborhood associations in post-Katrina New Orleans. In Faubourg Lafayette, the president said she was "thrown under the bus" when she was named president. In the Irish Channel, a former president remembered showing up late to an election meeting, only to find out she had been nominated and elected president in her absence. The paucity of volunteers for elected offices in associations gave those who did volunteer more power within the associations.

The aversion to volunteering reflects a harsh truth about neighborhood associations and activism. While much of the language of participation focuses on the uplifting experience of having an effect on the surrounding community, the reality is that most of the responsibility of participation falls on the shoulders of a few volunteers, and those volunteers quickly burn out, a pattern they share with their sister social-change organizations (Chetkovich and Kunreuther 2006). This burnout cycle is a process (Figure 4.1): neighborhood associations have a shortage of volunteers; they depend on crises to bring

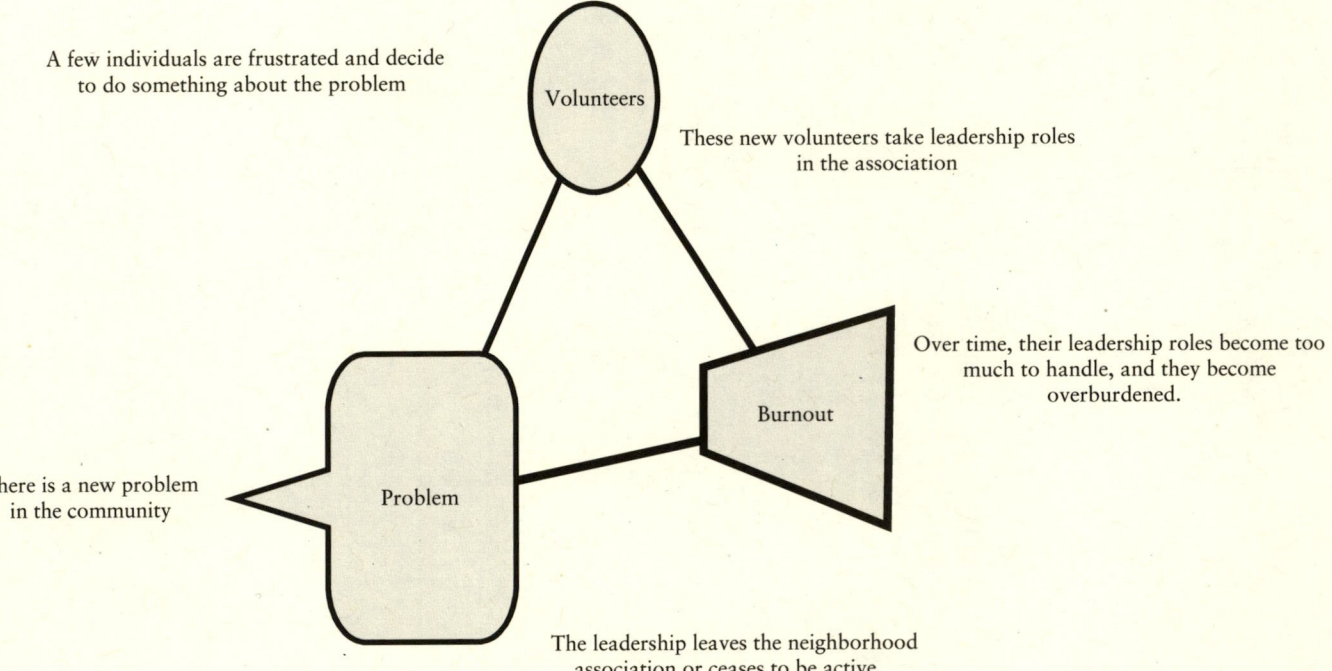

A few individuals are frustrated and decide
to do something about the problem

Volunteers

These new volunteers take leadership roles
in the association

There is a new problem
in the community

Problem

Burnout

Over time, their leadership roles become too
much to handle, and they become
overburdened.

The leadership leaves the neighborhood
association or ceases to be active.

Figure 4.1 The burnout cycle
A neighborhood crisis leads to increased volunteers, but the burden of volunteering leads to burnout.

volunteers into the fold; then, once in the fold, they become involved in a host of different issues, boards, and meetings (all unpaid), until they burn out and quit, leaving a gap for the next volunteer.

Even the Broadmoor Improvement Association suffers from volunteer burnout despite its relatively deep pool of volunteers and large budget. Figure 4.2 shows the many links the association has to other organizations. It has partnerships with the local Annunciation Church, Harvard University, and Bard College. It has spun off a number of nonprofits, including the Broadmoor Improvement District, the Broadmoor Community Development Corporation, and others. It is informally involved in the board of the local charter school. A core group of neighborhood volunteers serve across all of these related organizations. That same group is then called to represent the association at meetings with city planning, the police, or other agencies. As a result of these varied commitments, this core group is often in flux. Its members burn out, leaving the association short-handed and seeking new volunteers to throw into the fire.

The leadership of many associations in New Orleans was thinly spread across the boards of multiple organizations. In Pilotland, the relationship was enshrined. Corey, a pastor and the founder of the Pilotland Neighborhood Association, is adored by its members. One member said, "He's the man. Oh my God. He has the power. He's the spokesperson. We follow his lead." Corey was constantly juggling his role as a community leader and as a pastor. In Upper Audubon, Jerry was not only president of the association, but served on the board of the Upper Audubon Security District, which taxed itself to provide additional security to the neighborhood. The Lake Carmel Neighborhood Association had a similar relationship with the Lake Carmel Improvement District. In fact, the relationship was so close that the board often ignored the legal difference between the two organizations and held meetings and votes simultaneously. In Fontainebleau, Kerry served as the head of the Fontainebleau Improvement Association's crime committee, but also headed the legally separate Fontainebleau Security District, which collected voluntary funds to provide security to the neighborhood.

Many volunteers served on the boards of both their neighborhood association and its related security district. Other nonprofits drew from the same pool of volunteers as well. In Sugar Hill, neighborhood association leaders were connected to the Beacon of Hope and the Dillard University Community Development Corporation. In Algiers

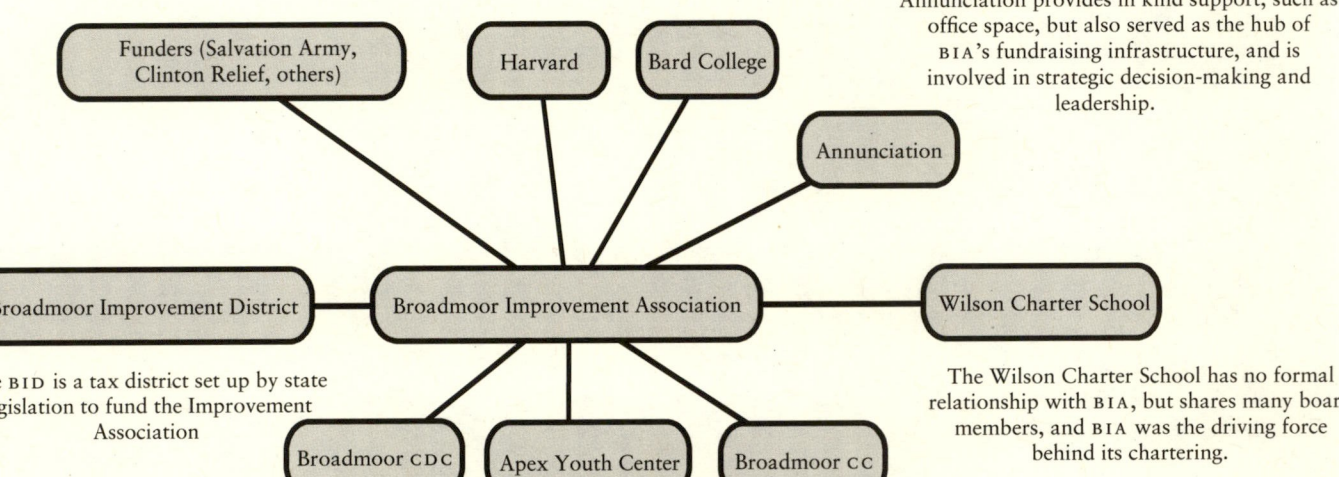

Broadmoor has had a host of funders to provide financial support, as well as volunteers.

Harvard and Bard College have long-term commitments that involve sending students as volunteers and providing technical and intellectual support. The schools also publish material on Post-Katrina New Orleans and can fundraise based on these New Orleans Initiatives.

Annunciation is the first partner of the BIA. Annunciation provides in kind support, such as office space, but also served as the hub of BIA's fundraising infrastructure, and is involved in strategic decision-making and leadership.

Funders (Salvation Army, Clinton Relief, others)

Harvard

Bard College

Annunciation

Broadmoor Improvement District

Broadmoor Improvement Association

Wilson Charter School

The BID is a tax district set up by state legislation to fund the Improvement Association

The Wilson Charter School has no formal relationship with BIA, but shares many board members, and BIA was the driving force behind its chartering.

Broadmoor CDC

Apex Youth Center

Broadmoor CC

The Broadmoor Community Development Corporation, Broadmoor Community Cares, and the Apex Youth Center are all funded by the Broadmoor Improvement Association. However, their leadership also serves on the board, and the legal entities are linked.

Figure 4.2 Broadmoor's partners
A visual representation of Broadmoor's complex governance network.

Point, key members of the Algiers Point Association founded Friends of the Ferry. In the Irish Channel, the association worked with the New Orleans Recreation Department to start the Lyons-Burke Booster Club to help fund local sports. Like the leaders of these associations, their volunteers were stretched thin by their commitments and this shaped the associations.

Burnout is a distortion of what Herbert (2005) calls neoliberal offloading. Herbert argues that burnout associated with local movements and nonprofits stems from the government pulling back from traditional services and depending on local organizations to fill the gap. In New Orleans, there is less offloading to neighborhood associations, but neighborhood leaders feel the same pressure through a different mechanism. Neighborhood associations are asked to participate in a multitude of processes. In some, they are an actual partner. In others, leaders serve as watchdogs to protect neighborhood interests. Throughout my time in New Orleans that reality was reflected through the constant debate over a Citizen Participation Plan (CPP) that had been brainstormed by Keith Twitchell and the Committee for a Better New Orleans. The plan addressed two of the key problems that led to burnout:

1 By formalizing neighborhood associations and their relationship to city hall, the CPP was designed to level the playing field by ensuring that less politically powerful associations got the same opportunities as politically well-connected associations. Ironically, this was one of the reasons the CPP was not enacted. It had to struggle to gain support from associations already happy with their access (and skeptical of the additional cost of the CPP to get what they already had).

2 The CPP included an "Early Notification System" that established a legal requirement that city government ensured that neighborhood associations received timely information about development, planning, and zoning changes in their communities. The idea was to avoid what became known colloquially among neighborhood activists as "planning by surprise," in which a neighborhood leader would learn at the last minute about a meeting on controversial changes to the neighborhood's zoning plan or something similar.

Too often, neighborhood associations found themselves scrambling at the last minute to rally residents to attend city meetings in support of a neighborhood position on development. Associations became used to a host of different avoidance tactics practiced by local government and proponents of a particular development. Meetings were announced at the last minute. Items were tabled until subsequent meetings, meaning that neighborhood residents would have to show up at multiple meetings to oppose or support a project. Worse still, even at zoning board meetings, city planning meetings, or historical preservation committee meetings, neighborhood associations had no formal role; it was left to the discretion of board members to "listen" to neighborhood associations.

Kristen, the president of the Northwest Carrolton Neighborhood Association, describes the first few years after the storm as a process of learning about the intricacies of city bureaucracy, constantly having to learn the who and the how of change. Neighborhood associations had to have connections to city agencies to learn about changes in their neighborhoods. They also had to do the research necessary to convince various boards to deny changes proposed by developers (or side with them on other issues), which often involved navigating the confusing legal standards by which various boards could approve or deny projects and then showing up with enough force at the appropriate meeting to make sure their arguments were heard. That happened across a multitude of systems. Neighborhood associations opposed development, rallied and recruited developers, kept on top of changes to police beats, contributed testimony to code enforcement hearings, and gathered data for blight remediation, among many other activities. To be a neighborhood association president was to be on top of all of these processes and to be the person who does this research and attends these meetings when the rest of the neighborhood residents are too exhausted to do so.

Given the immense pressure, burnout is inevitable, and it is no wonder that associations find volunteers hard to come by. These realities put a different face on democratic mechanisms, such as participatory budgeting, within the right to the city (see de Souza, 2001). Lefebvre (1943), Purcell (2002), and Harvey (2012) do not explain the mechanisms by which this right is enabled. But the informal system in New Orleans is clearly a stopgap – neighborhood associations struggle with finding the resources, time, and volunteers to fulfill their end of the participation bargain. Worse still, these pressures result in a version of the local trap, empowering those with the time, energy, and inclination to volunteer. For those who do volunteer, the bargain is equally poor. As Louise, the executive director of the Vieux Carré Property Owners, Residents, and Associates, put it, "If I have to participate one more time, I'm going to scream." Such a system puts democratic pressure on neighborhood associations. The issue is not as simple as empowering neighborhoods with more resources and social capital; it concerns the individuals within them who have the time to work across multiple city processes.

The fundamental reality of a neighborhood association is that it needs a core group of volunteers willing to do a tremendous amount of work. This pressure warps not just the lives of activists, who quickly burn out, but also the strategies of the associations themselves. Neighborhood associations have developed specific strategies to stretch resources and volunteers. They amplify the voices of as few as one or two residents to ensure that they become dedicated volunteers. They spin off organizations to address specific issues in the neighborhood, a strategy that has the potential to increase the volunteer base and keep the neighborhood association nimble. This often has the double effect of ensuring that the associations stretch the same limited volunteer base across additional positions and responsibilities and reach out to and recruit nonprofits and governmental agencies to provide services that the associations are unable to provide, a tactic that allows them to stretch limited resources. But each of these strategies impacts the primary role of an association – to be a democratic representative for the neighborhood.

Several associations vocalized a strategy that involved putting the full force of the neighborhood behind specific individuals in order to get those individuals to volunteer and lead initiatives in the neighborhood. Ulysses from French Quarters Citizens Inc. utilized this model when he had his neighborhood association act as a "megaphone." In the megaphone model, a neighborhood association will champion any issue that as few as one or two people care about if they will volunteer to lead the initiative. But for Ulysses, amplifying the concerns of individual residents was both desirable and logical. He thought that the purpose of a neighborhood association was to give each individual resident more power. Thus, if a resident had a reasonable complaint, the association should put the entire weight of the neighborhood behind the issue.

Anna learned the same lesson when newly elected president of the Irish Channel Neighborhood Association. Her motivation for volunteering was to convince the association to offer more sports programs in Annunciation Park so that her five-year-old son would have organized play. She also thought sports programs were a proactive way to address crime issues in the community. At the same time, other association members thought more crime prevention and protection were needed, as a spat of murders in the neighborhood had convinced many of the neighbors that they needed a neighborhood watch. Anna worried that a neighborhood watch would stoke fears in the neighborhood, but she decided that it was not worth the effort to fight that initiative. If supporters of the neighborhood watch could find the volunteers, they were more than welcome to run it. She came to see her role as a neighborhood association leader, one who would support initiatives that had enough volunteer capital to run. So the neighborhood watch, which combined the leadership of a former policemen with the association's "old guard" and which focused on crime issues, became a reality despite her reservations.

The megaphone model was evident on many different levels. In the French Quarter, Bill used the megaphone himself, leading a task force to investigate illegal renting in the neighborhood. It was an issue that he was particularly concerned about as the owner of a small hotel. In Upper Audubon, the association put together an oral history of the neighborhood, taking advantage of a local historian's skills. In Broadmoor, their dynamic president, Latoya Cantrell, focused on the issues she knew best, creating an education corridor and helping to run the local school.

These realities put a different face on the New Orleans neighborhood movement. While a powerful activist tool, in practice the movement does not underpin a new urban utopia. It is a stopgap, one that residents are willing to support as long as the threat level in the neighborhood is high. Neighborhood activism is less a right and more a tool of last resort. For those who volunteer, the risk of burnout is high and the challenges of maintaining such involvement are myriad. A permanent politics of inhabitants that depends on neighborhood activists threatens to entrench elements of neoliberalism with "offloading" from the state to neighborhoods, and neighborhoods themselves struggle to balance the interests of the neighborhood with potentially exclusionary instincts.

At first glance, such politics appears to be a stinging indictment of neighborhood associations. Over and over, these associations attend government meetings and participate as representatives of a local neighborhood despite their own questionable democratic underpinnings. Yet, in urban communities, many of these same complaints can be leveled at traditional democratic institutions. Logan (2006) writes that after Hurricane Katrina, voting in the mayoral election saw predictable drops of close to 10 per cent compared to pre-storm elections in 2002 and 40 per cent less than what Logan calls "potential turnout" – that is, compared to the November 2004 national election. Worse still, the drop in voter turnout was not evenly distributed across races. After the storm, blacks as a share of the electorate dropped 6 to 7 per cent. However, in predominantly black New Orleans East, voter turnout fell by 23 per cent, while in the Lower Ninth Ward it fell by nearly 40 per cent. Dahl (1961) writes about the traditional role that business leaders and elites have in urban politics, one that was reflected in New Orleans when business leaders attempted to rally support for a whiter, wealthier city. Just as neighborhood democracy is plagued by systems that privilege groups with more resources and power over others, city politics does the same. The metaphor of a backroom filled with cigar smoke as political powers negotiate can be an apt one for city politics. The Jefferson Parish black community still bears the scars of the decision – pushed by bankers and prominent businessmen in New Orleans – to blow the levees and flood the largely black surrounding parish during the flood of 1927 (see Barry 1998). The backroom metaphor can also be applied to neighborhood associations. The president of the Fontainebleau Improvement Association explains that his association knows where to go in the city: "We're like a mini city council office" and when there are problems, "we'll make the right calls and get it done." That theme of knowing where to go within government bureaucracy is critical and easier for a neighborhood such as Fontainebleau, in which the association president would eventually take a position promoting New Orleans tourism.

Associations with fewer personal ties to city administration struggled to be their own "mini city council office" rather than have to depend directly on actual city council offices. Such partnerships manifested in almost every neighborhood in my sample, even though many of the issues that neighborhood associations focus on, including crime, blight, development and infrastructure, do not come directly under the purview of the city council but are instead largely handled by other administrative offices within the mayoral administration. To make things odder, the council and associations appear at times to be competing for legitimacy as representatives of their communities.

But these relationships are often mutually beneficial. City council officers have come to depend on information from neighborhood associations, while for neighborhood associations, city council officers have become necessary advocates to ensure that work in their neighborhood gets done in a timely manner.

A city council staffer who did constituent services in Gentilly called this the "bump up" system. At the time, the system for fixing potholes, replacing street lights, or getting permits was "completely arbitrary. It was like the Wild West." Sometimes the Safety and Permits Office was doing work via handwritten notes walked to the office by city council staffers. As a result, each of these city services, which in most cities are dealt with within a few days, had waiting lists. Neighborhood associations would call in favors and lobby to try to get bumped up on these lists. Those with fewer favors to call in and fewer connections in government bureaucracy developed relationships with the local city council members' office, which would then lobby the appropriate agency. The staffer explaining the bump-up system did not view this as a corrupt process. Instead, he emphasized that city agencies struggled to do their jobs effectively. That left neighborhood associations to play a watchdog function, keeping track of their submissions and projects, and the city council's role was that of a catalyst for action because "every once in a while there is an error in the department." The bump up-system shows the sharp dichotomy brought about by systems that require participation. However, there is the opportunity for political favoritism and a clear preference that neighborhoods be organized. But the daily experience of this system is more complicated. The bump-up system is greased not by bribes, but by obsessive neighborhood leaders who will not leave bureaucrats alone until issues in their neighborhood are addressed.

That still leads to equity questions, but the categories of powerful and effective associations have the same cognitive dissonance. The strongest neighborhood associations are not just those in the richest neighborhoods, as there needs to be a threat that inspires the time of persnickety volunteers willing to call a city council office every day until something is addressed – an approach that a former president of the Irish Channel Neighborhood Association freely admitted to. For some of New Orleans's wealthiest neighborhoods, the absence of threats means that while the associations may have the potential to bump up neighborhood problems, the problems do not exist. Take, for example, the Upper Audubon Association. The association rarely comes up in debates around the city, despite an average home value that one resident insisted was in the $2 million range (a number the president of the association contested, calling the average home value just north of $1 million). The neighborhood describes itself as "upper, upper middle income" on a nice day and as "elitist" if feeling slightly more critical. The association has a very narrow approach towards activism. Its president insists that it deals with "only things that have a direct impact on Upper Audubon." The main focus of the association is its security district. One resident thought that was because "they don't have to concern themselves with quality of life" and that "they're so elitist that they don't need anything." Here, Boyte's (1980) idea that localities compete by providing better services comes to life. The residents of Upper Audubon have chosen the neighborhood in part because the quality of life is so high that they do not have to fight and scrap for attention to fix neighborhood issues.

That same pattern manifests itself in the Fontainebleau Improvement Association. Even though the association has comparatively more resources and more social capital in city government, it has few places to assert that capacity. Association leaders admit to lacking "a galvanizing issue" in part because "we weren't a target" after the storm when the Green Dot Plan suggested that some neighborhoods become parks. Fontainebleau has primary schools and even a university in its neighborhood. Its residents can walk to local shopping opportunities, bars, and even a grocery store (though that story is complex and will be examined in Chapter 5). Why go through the grueling process of being a neighborhood association leader when there is so little to address in the community?

The third high-income neighborhood in the study sample is the French Quarter, with its two major associations: French Quarter Citizens Inc. and the Vieux Carré Property Owners, Residents, and Associates (VCPORA). The French Quarter faces a distinct threat to residents' way of life. The neighborhood draws over seven million tourists each year (McNulty 2012). This impacts the daily lives of residents in innumerable ways. If a French Quarter resident leaves a trash can outside after trash removal, tourists passing by inevitably fill it with trash: beer cups, gum, a leftover po'boy. Local bars pipe music through speakers out open windows, a practice that may attract tourists but drives local residents crazy. "Barkers" for restaurants or bars are a similar nuisance in daily life. They often follow tourists (or residents), urging them to enter an establishment. Again, for the tourist, this is a momentary annoyance. For a resident, it is an everyday hassle. As a result, both associations in the Quarter have focused heavily on quality of life legislation, and according to Ulysses, the French Quarter Inc. president, that has largely been a success. The more difficult struggle has been ensuring enforcement. At the French Quarter Citizens Inc. annual meeting, the New Orleans Police Department chief, Ronald Serpass, spoke. This was part of a wider campaign to get police to enforce quality of life legislation, including noise violations. But there are plenty of intermediary steps to such enforcement, such as convincing police that, given wider issues like the violent crime in the city, resources and time would best be spent enforcing quality of life provisions. An active member of French Quarter Citizens Inc. argues that "[e]nforcement doesn't work here, it may work some other places, but it doesn't work here." She cites the lack of noise meters owned by the police: "How can the police enforce decibel limits when its officers do not even have the proper equipment to measure noise on the street?"

There is a wider conversation of importance here, that of NIMBY-ism more broadly and specifically the question of whether prioritizing local quality of life can lead to exclusion. These neighborhood associations clearly feel threatened. They are looking over their shoulders. When a proposal surfaced to create a French Quarter tax district to raise money for extra services in the neighborhood, VCPORA opposed it even though French Quarter Citizens Inc. and VCPORA would have had seats on the board. But according to the VCPORA executive director, the associations would only have had four or five of the thirteen residential seats. Given the immense pressure from businesses and the opportunity for profit, the associations were concerned that businesses could infiltrate the residential board. In fact, developers had long since bought property along nearby Rampart Street, then lobbied for changes in zoning that would make it more like Bourbon Street and dramatically altered resale values as bars and clubs could now build on the street. Because of similar concerns, VCPORA does not hold elections, using an executive director model rather than a democratic one.

These associations feel threatened and describe themselves as reactionary. That is a radical difference from the Fontainebleau Improvement Association and the Upper Audubon Association. Those associations, without threats, need little influence on a daily basis. French Quarters Citizens Inc. and VCPORA need more power to protect their neighborhood. The intersection of threat, potential for resources, and volunteers passionate about their cause is part of the reason the two associations are among the most powerful in the state. It also connects directly to Hajer's (2003) argument that activism is often responsive, not creative. He uses the hypothetical of a park slated to be turned over to development. In this hypothetical, activists react to the news by putting up an empty frame, a symbolic act of resistance that reminds us of the beauty of the park and of what the community already has. He argues that we tend to think of these activists as influencing the decision of whether to preserve the land as a park or develop it. But they just as easily could be responding to that decision. According to Haas (1977), this responsive/creative ambiguity is particularly true in post-disaster contexts, when residents naturally focus on the pre-disaster city as a model for its redevelopment. That combination of crisis and desire to return to the city is a powerful motivator for associations, and it works not only for upper-class neighborhoods, but also for struggling neighborhoods with fewer resources.

Take the Sugar Hill Neighborhood as an example. The Sugar Hill Neighborhood Association is little more than two dedicated residents, Tammy and Maria. The largely black neighborhood is tucked into a strange corner of Gentilly, cut off on multiple sides by the exit ramps connecting North Broad Street to I-610, railroad tracks, and the London Canal. As a result, as in many Gentilly neighborhoods, the residents feel left out of the broader recovery process. A seemingly small issue motivated Tammy's involvement in her association. After Hurricane Katrina, the US Postal Service ceased individual mail delivery in her neighborhood. At first, the Postal Service said that not enough people had returned to the neighborhood. So Tammy and a few friends counted their neighbors to prove how many had returned. Then the Postal Service said that it could not deliver mail because it did not know which houses were occupied. So Tammy went door-to-door and gathered that information. Then, the Postal Service said that too many mailboxes had been damaged in the storm and there was nowhere to put the mail. So Tammy helped make sure every house had its own mailbox. All of this, according to her, was just because "I just got tired of going across the street to get my mail in the mud" and "people shouldn't have to pay taxes and walk to their house in boots."

Associations and activists with distinct threats and crises often bind together to enable change. But this process is more difficult without the resources and human capital of a wealthier neighborhood. Wealth, in dozens of tiny ways, props up activism. It allows parents to pay for child care so that they can attend a meeting. It supports families with one non-working parent who will be able to volunteer during free time. White-collar jobs are more likely to be forgiving of a long lunch break for a meeting at city hall than a blue-collar job paid by the hour, when a long lunch break may be the difference between meeting rent and eviction. These individual limitations flow into what can be an overwhelming number of issues in a neighborhood.

For the Pilotland neighborhood, something as simple as establishing a relationship with the city council was challenging. Pilotland's leaders make a point of saying that the neighborhood is historical and among the first neighborhoods where blacks could purchase a home but had no association at the time of the storm. The city council's office had done blight tours in most neighborhoods in the district, but because the office was unaware of Pilotland or its fledgling association, the neighborhood had been skipped. As a result, it was years behind in processes such as code enforcement or even simpler infrastructure issues like replacing broken lights or filling potholes. Despite all this, there are a wide variety of issues in the neighborhood, from child care to quality of life to the need for educational institutions and commercial businesses. The association is designed primarily to deal with quality of life issues, and an economic development corporation was launched to help jumpstart development in the neighborhood. The neighborhood depends on the local church to address services and poverty. But those organizations are led by the same person, further stretching the time of that individual and limiting the capacity of the association. Even before the storm, Pilotland experienced disinvestment. After the storm, the neighborhood had no pharmacy, no health clinic, no dental clinic, no fresh produce, and no community center. Without a pre-existing relationship with the city council, without the name recognition of New Orleans's more recognizable neighborhoods, and without a stable of volunteers to address these issues, the neighborhoods' challenges were overwhelming.

The power and capacity of neighborhood associations is mediated not only by income but also by threat level. Wealthy neighborhoods have the potential (resources and volunteers) to be powerful but often lack the existential threat to the neighborhood that would necessitate involvement. Low-income neighborhoods are faced with the opposite, sometimes overwhelming needs but lack the capacity to pursue them.

In the middle lie most associations, with resources stretched and neighborhood needs immediate. For these associations, the bump-up system is a necessary evil. It is a neighborhood politics of last resort. Neighborhood activists would rather these crises not touch their homes. They would rather not have to sacrifice their time and energy to participate. A city council staffer expressed hope that the burden on such activists might be lessened. New Orleans Mayor Mitch Landrieu, for example, was in the process of overhauling the "311" reporting system for blight, road maintenance, street lights, and beyond. But while the bump-up system could be solved with more effective local governance, the wider movement towards participation indicates that this bump-up dynamic is likely to continue. Neighborhood associations exist to defend local interests, and the movement towards informal participatory influence means associations get involved, even if doing so puts pressure on residents and leads to eventual burnout.

Given that the New Orleans neighborhood movement was a politics of last resort, neighborhood associations have developed numerous strategies for addressing local issues and working around local governance, all while trying to avoid stretching the volunteer base too thin. That effort reflects the lessons of Piven and Cloward (1979), who argue that organizations that become formal frequently lose their ability to take decisive and radical action, and in doing so, limit their own effectiveness, but it contradicts Polletta (2002), which finds an increase in the rules and formal mechanisms in social movements practicing participatory democracy. One strategy that neighborhood associations use to maintain flexibility and informality is to reorient the association to give potential volunteers the its full-throated support (Ulysses's megaphone model). Another is to join city council or other agencies to try to bump delayed neighborhood projects to the top of the waiting list. A third strategy is to create spin-off organizations to help keep neighborhood associations relatively nimble and prevent the association from playing the primary role in a major crisis (while avoiding, at the same time, having other issues fall through the cracks during a crisis). This strategy has been used across a number of examples in this study. In Algiers Point, facing the potential closing of the Algiers Ferry, the Algiers Point Association created Friends of the Ferry, which focused explicitly on that issue. The spin-off occurred at a time when many new members were coming to association meetings to talk about the ferry. Strategically, the spin-off was good politics, allowing residents who wanted to be sure the ferry would continue to run to appear as a coalition. It also meant that the association's focus on local crime issues would not get drowned out by the fervor over the ferry. The Broadmoor Improvement Association followed a similar model in spinning off the Broadmoor Improvement District, the Broadmoor CDC, Broadmoor Community Cares, and the Apex Youth Center.

A host of associations, such as the Upper Audubon Association and the Lake Carmel Civic Improvement Association, created spin-off security districts. These districts were funded by a neighborhood tax. The Fontainebleau Improvement Association created the Fontainebleau Security District, which collects voluntary donations from homeowners. Each of these security paraphernalia are technically separate entities (for legal purposes as well) but have overlapping leadership. In the cases of Lake Carmel and Fontainebleau, many of the meetings are held the same evening so that volunteers can attend both meetings. The Irish Channel spun off the Lyons-Burke Booster Club to raise money for its sports programs. French Quarter Citizens Inc. is actually a VCPORA spin-off to focus more directly on residential quality of life. Later, North Rampart Main Street Inc. would split from French Quarter Citizens Inc. to focus more directly on Rampart Street and the possibility of streetcar runs expanding there. In Gentilly, the Dreux Avenue Good Neighbors Society split from the Gentilly Terrace and Gardens Neighborhood Association to focus more explicitly on its block. These strategies should be seen as explicit strategies both to keep neighborhood associations lithe and nimble and to increase power by making a coalition appear wider and deeper in a community.

The strategy also comes with a downside. Creating a spin-off organization does not necessarily widen the volunteer base and it can exacerbate problems with burnout. It is an effective way for organizations to stay mission-driven and keep from over-expanding, but it comes at a cost. The organization stays lithe, but the same volunteer base is stretched even further because associations often fall back to the same core group of volunteers when staffing these new organizations. The head of the security committee in the Fontainebleau Improvement Association is the same individual who directs the Fontainebleau Security District. Lake Carmel and Upper Audubon have similar overlaps. In Broadmoor, the Broadmoor Improvement District's elected officials included representatives from other spin-offs, such as the Apex Community Center. And when Broadmoor's new charter school struggled with test scores, the board was reconfigured to include more residents from the association.

This is not the only strategy associations use to expand their influence without overwhelming small organizations. Another strategy is to limit meetings and elections and keep a low profile through times with few neighborhood crises. In Sugar Hill, Tammy and Maria have moved away from holding regular meetings, largely because so few people attend. Rather than use up precious volunteer capital on planning and attending regular meetings, the association chooses to focus volunteer hours on specific initiatives and partnerships. The Northwest Carrollton Neighborhood Association has eschewed more-formal elections for much the same reason.

In many associations, there is a natural rhythm to the association's activism. In the Upper Audubon Association, a proposal by Tulane to build dorms in the Uptown Square led to a quick response, followed by a ramp-up of neighborhood activities prior to Hurricane Katrina. But when that project was scrapped after the storm, instead of continuing to ramp up its activities, the association naturally became smaller and more lithe. In Coliseum Square, the same pattern manifested itself as opposition to a public housing project, and scatter-site housing animated the neighborhood, which saw a decline in membership and activity in the years when there was not such a controversial issue.

Neighborhood associations increase the numbers of individual volunteers, create spin-off organizations, choose to swell in size during crisis and shrink without it, all as a way of dealing with the lack of resources and volunteers that associations face as they attempt to protect and improve their neighborhoods. But perhaps the most effective strategy is to find partners to work in the neighborhood. No neighborhood used this strategy more effectively than Sugar Hill.

The strategy developed by Tammy and Maria for the Sugar Hill Neighborhood Association was twofold. They wanted to be visible, and they wanted to increase organizational capacity beyond their ability to volunteer by taking advantage of the services provided by partner organizations. The unofficial motto of the pair was, "The only way you can be visible is to be visible." So, they joined boards, showed up at meetings, and made sure that if an initiative was started to help neighborhoods after the storm, Sugar Hill was on the list of beneficiaries. The result was that an association with low member involvement, very few volunteers, and perhaps few members had a large footprint. Tammy and Maria could point outside to a boulevard project made possible by a grant they won; they participated in health clinics, enacted broken windows strategies such as getting new signage for the neighborhood, and co-hosted computer training for residents. All of these things were what the two called a "chain reaction" to being active and present at meetings with other organizations. It was a strategy of partnership in action. The Sugar Hill Neighborhood Association provides a model for other neighborhood associations. Because associations are low capacity, in terms of both dollars and volunteers, one way to ramp up their efforts is to partner with groups that are working on similar priorities.

Many of the partnerships already described here fit this model. The Northwest Carrollton Neighborhood Association, the Gentilly Terrace and Gardens Association, the Fontainebleau Improvement Association, the Irish-Channel Association, and, yes, the Sugar Hill Neighborhood Association partnered with Parkway or Hike 4 Katreena to plant new trees in their neighborhoods. The Irish Channel Neighborhood Association partnered with the New Orleans Recreation Department to offer youth sports in local parks.

Similar pairings occurred throughout the city. A host of nonprofits thrived in these symbiotic relationships, addressing blight, planting trees, and providing extra security to help fill neighborhood needs. Different academic voices look at relationships such as these and try to understand and differentiate them. Lawson (2002) talks about integrated relationships and explains that they can co-locate, communicate, coordinate, and converge. Others expand to include categories such as informal relationships, integrative relationships, convergent relationships, and others (Hogue 1993; Cigler 2001; Leutz 1999; and Szirom et al. 2002).

Provan and Kenis (2008) highlight the need to understand not just the outcome of networks, but also how they function. Distinguishing types of relationships within networks helps us to do that. Brown and Keast (2003) settle for just "three Cs": collaboration, cooperation, and coordination. In doing so, they build on other theorists (Winer and Ray 1994; Konrad 1996; and Fine 2001). Underpinning these categories are two factors: the length of the relationships and the extent of sharing responsibility/resources in the partnership.

Breaking down relationships into length and depth makes them easier to understand. Nonprofits such as Hike 4 Katreena and Parkway engage in one-off activities that share resources and responsibility with neighborhood associations. Brown and Keast (2003) call this coordination because it involves shared planning and decision-making

(Mulford and Rogers 1982; Daka-Mulwanda 1995; Lawson 2002). Such coordination often is for a single goal or activity (Litterer 1973; Lawson 2002). Partnerships, such as the one between the Irish Channel Neighborhood Association and the New Orleans Recreation Department, take this coordination a step forward. By sharing vision and responsibilities for the long-term, they engage in what Brown and Keast (2003) call collaboration. Similarly, Tammy and Maria's Sugar Hill strategy is one of cultivating long-term, collaborative relationships in order to expand the capacity of their association. In an analysis of seventy-one different partnerships with neighborhood associations 52 per cent fell into these two categories: collaborative and coordinative. Lacking the funding or volunteers to build their own programming, associations relied heavily on these types of partnerships as a way to pursue their mission. Many of these partnerships depended on mutual need.

Another popular partner, Kaboom!, builds playgrounds in communities and has become an explicitly symbiotic model. Neighborhoods must provide local volunteers and help fund projects. But the nonprofit provides the design and expertise, matches funding, and coordinates the day designated to build the facility. Local communities are then invested and motivated to help maintain the property. This same pattern is the core of many relationships, from youth programs to tree planting, from health fairs to computer literacy programs. Nonprofits require connections and buy-ins from communities, and joining a neighborhood association is often one of the best ways to connect to local residents.

The mutual need with political figures is more complex and contains more space for tokenism in participation. Kristen, from the Northwest Carrollton Neighborhood Association, calls this the "Faustian Bargain" in which neighborhood associations get the ear of local politicians, and in return associations come to meetings so that politicians "can say they have butts in chairs." In other words, access is a condition of ensuring that politicians look as though they are popular in neighborhoods. This can drift dangerously close to what Arnstein (1969) describes as tokenism in her ladder of participation. Part of the frustration of neighborhood leaders across the city is the way in which participation can devolve into political theater, providing cover for politicians (see Arnold 1979).

Education activists in New Orleans learned this lesson. Paul Vallas and Paul Pastorek, the two architects of the dramatic changes to education that took place in New Orleans, did so by bluntly wielding state power. They expanded the Recovery School District, a state-run school district that took over schools with low test scores, and in doing so, attempted a radical experiment that would eventually be the nation's first all-charter school district (Layton 2014). Vallas and Pastorek were not elected officials and were notorious for their heavy-handed approach. Not surprisingly there were no votes about the changes to the education system. The African-American community most directly affected by the changes was frustrated because so many teachers from their community were fired while young, gentrifying "outsiders" (usually white) replaced them in the new schools. So, when John White took the position of superintendent of the Recovery School District, one of his first moves was to do a listening tour through New Orleans neighborhoods. Such tours have since become standard practice in education circles, and they were recently repeated by Paymon Rouhanifard in Camden, NJ (Davis 2014), and by Pamela Brown in Buffalo, NY (Buckley 2014). But what was most interesting about John White's listening tour was that it did very little to change the direction of the school district. White was listening, but not acting, on the things he heard.

Mayor Mitch Landrieu played from the same script when he established town hall meetings about his budgets. The meetings were great theater (the mayor himself was a theater major in college). Landrieu brought his staff and the heads of many departments to the town hall meeting. When the audience raised questions about public works or other budget items, Landrieu brought the corresponding department head onstage to answer the questions. The crowd loved the meetings, Landrieu loved the theater, and the town halls got such good reviews that the mayor not only made them an annual event, but used them as impetus to create the Neighborhood Engagement Office. And yet, those familiar with the budgetary process insisted that the budget had been written prior to the town halls and that little had structurally changed within it. On the margins, a project might be added or dropped, but the meetings were more important to the mayor for the public support they garnered for him than for debate over the budget.

There is a fine line between engagement and tokenism. Listening does not ensure action. On the other hand, the need for access to politicians and to resources from nonprofits can undermine the democratic nature of neighborhood associations themselves. For a neighborhood like Pilotland, having an association is necessary to get on the agenda of the local city council. In Faubourg Lafayette, a case we will examine more closely in Chapter 5, a city council officer specifically asked two mothers to form a neighborhood association to give the impression their advocacy was supported by the entire neighborhood. "Hiding behind letterhead" is not just a critique of neighborhood associations, it is a critique of a wider ecosystem that craves the stamp of approval from authentic neighborhood associations so much that it will at times support associations despite having limited democratic credentials.

This is the importance of examining the New Orleans neighborhood movement and its parallels (and differences) in our understanding of the right to the city. In post-Katrina New Orleans, residents worried that policy experts would overwhelm both local perspectives and local needs. It was a script that played out in post-storm planning, when the Green Dot Plan recommended a reduced footprint that would relocate those who had already struggled to return to flooded neighborhoods. It was a script that played out in health care as residents fought over the reopening of Charity Hospital. It was a script that played out in housing, over the demolition of the Lafitte housing project. And it was a script that played out in education as a school system with neighborhood schools was replaced largely by open-enrollment charter schools. In each of these policy shifts there was an aspect of localism. Residents were activated in response to policy (see Hajer 2003) and, like many residents in post-disaster contexts, they gravitated towards the city as it was before the storm (Haas 1977). Yet, as scholars have pointed out (see Arena 2012; Buras 2014; Adams 2013) each of these policies also has a neoliberal bent to them. From education to housing, health care to urban planning, the focus has been on infusing market logic into policy. In this way, the New Orleans neighborhood movement has manifested itself almost exactly as laid out by Purcell (2008) – a local democratic movement has become a bastion of defense against neoliberalism.

But that reduction is over-simplistic. The demand for participation bends electoral politics and warps the way associations act. Associations have responsibilities in a host of different policy networks, providing evidence for code enforcement, data about blighted housing, input for community policing, and even help in crowd-sourcing the municipal budget. That demand puts tremendous pressure on associations and ultimately undermines their ability to be democratic.

Serving as president of a neighborhood association is a thankless task. It involves keeping track of dozens of simultaneous neighborhood issues, skipping work for meetings, coming home late for even more meetings, all the while having little actual power in policy processes. Just finding enough volunteers to conduct neighborhood business is a difficult task. As a result, neighborhood associations themselves warp to maintain themselves. They throw their weight behind individual residents who serve as a megaphone for individuals' strong opinions, anything to attract new and dedicated volunteers. They create spin-off organizations to make sure that neighborhood associations are not overwhelmed by single issues, but still stretch a limited volunteer pool further. They partner closely with nonprofits to stretch resources, but in doing so, can come to represent not just residents but also nonprofit organizations. And they have a political role in the electoral process, where they receive access in return for giving elected officials the much-needed appearance of community support. Each of these coping mechanisms changes and challenges the orthodox interpretation of the neighborhood movement as being a democratic anchor opposed to neoliberalism.

In a vacuum, many of these critiques directly undermine the idea that these associations are democratic. But neighborhood associations do not exist in a vacuum. They exist in real political contexts that have already-entrenched structures with democratic flaws of their own. The lobbying of associations to bump up neighborhood projects in the queues of city agencies takes place in the context of waiting lists that other influential individuals or organizations already manipulate. The very demand for participation exists only because local politics can become so divorced from local communities that residents seek another power base for opposition. The New Orleans neighborhood movement and its selective embrace of the right to the city is a neighborhood politics of last resort. Residents would rather not volunteer. They would rather not have to participate and attend meeting after meeting just to defend their communities. These neighborhood activists are not motivated by the belief that a neighborhood system is ideal, but rather by the apprehension that traditional systems are failing to represent their interests. As such, they create what Chaskin and Garg (1997) call a "parallel system." The neighborhood associations system is likely a temporary solution (neighborhoods struggle to maintain the necessary core of volunteers, and the system is predicated on local crises) but it is a necessary one, given existing institutions' failure to defend neighborhood interests. This undermines the ability of associations to be democratic; they have neither the sanction nor the resources of traditional democratic institutions. Yet the system echoes much of the recent literature on democratic theory. Some deliberative democratic theorists suggest that deliberation sans self-interest can improve democratic outcomes (Gutmann and Thompson 2002), while others argue that ugly and informal conflicts impose themselves on real-life democracy (Dodge 2009). Polletta (2002, 1–2) turns this argument inside out, arguing that while "[c]onventional wisdom has it that participatory democracy is worthy in principle but unwieldy in practice," "[a]ctivists in every major movement of the last hundred years have found strategic value in participatory democratic decision making." The discussion of democratic justice within the right to the city reflects the same tension. Attoh (2011) writes that there is a split in right to the city theorists; some such as Busà (2009), Ascher (2009), and Angotti (2009), frame the right to the city in terms of democratic participation. Harvey (2008) goes a step further, arguing that there must be democratic management. Other scholars, though, such as Mitchell (2003), frame the right to the city specifically in terms of protection of vulnerable communities from the majority. The informality of these concepts of participation and rights contributes to this messiness – there is a need for participation and protection, but when specific organizations fill that need, they bring with them their own democratic challenges.

New Orleans neighborhood associations are no exception. Neighborhood associations have power not because of their purity as democratic institutions. They are severely flawed. But in a political context in dire need of local participation, neighborhood associations have stepped in to that gap to fill local demand both on behalf of residents and government. The neighborhood movement manifests itself as a neighborhood politics of last resort. It is a temporary solution. It is a system that "burns out" its volunteers and struggles with the balance between holding elected officials accountable and needing to cozy up to them to receive beneficial treatment. It is a politics of last resort.

♦

5

Can NIMBYs Fight for Justice?

I think the tension between homeowners and renters only becomes
apparent when management fails.

Becky, founder of the Historic Faubourg Lafayette
Neighborhood Association

You are what's wrong with this city.

A patron of the Community Book Center, the oldest
African-American-owned bookstore in the city

New, old, black, Hispanic. It's everything, and it's one big gumbo
that's delicious.

Jeannette, former president of the Irish
Channel Neighborhood Association

The "hiding behind letterhead" critique of neighborhood associations is one of legitimacy. It deals with the fundamental question of
whether associations truly represent their neighborhoods. But there
is a deeper critique that deals not with what associations are, but
with what they do. This critique moves beyond their intentions and
priorities, beyond their partnerships and ideals, to ask the following
question: can neighborhood associations be just in their activism?
This issue of justice stems from the reputation that neighborhood
associations have of screaming "Not in my backyard" when faced
with everything from commercial development to affordable housing. Neighborhood associations have gained the potential not only to
limit economic development, but also to discriminate against vulnerable populations and people of color. NIMBYism is the ugly side of
the neighborhood movement's embrace of elements of the right
to the city. Does empowering local geographic units mean giving

neighborhoods with more resources and fewer people of color the right to discriminate against those with fewer resources and darker skin hues?

I saw NIMBYism up close in the Faubourg St Johns neighborhood. There, the neighborhood association discussed a closed local nursing home that had been purchased by a nonprofit for renovation as a facility for homeless transitional housing. The surrounding neighborhood associations and members of Faubourg St Johns Neighborhood Association were split in their views on the project, and a local zoning ordinance that required a certain number of parking spots for each resident in a dwelling became the focal point of the battle. The nonprofit renovating the facility sought a waiver of the parking ordinance, and some neighborhood associations in the surrounding community opposed that waiver. Such opposition made little sense on its face. The parking spots requirement was designed to keep the neighborhood from having a parking shortage, but the transitioning homeless could hardly be expected to have cars. The opposition was not about parking spaces.

One local resident became particularly agitated during an association meeting. He opposed an influx of homeless people into his neighborhood, and the parking issue was the only grounds for opposition to the project, which otherwise complied with zoning regulations. However, the underlying concerns he addressed at public meetings related to the presence of homeless individuals. Was it safe to bring so many homeless into the community? Why should his community have to have the facility? Would his children be hassled by homeless men?

After the meeting I spoke to two different activists who gave me opposing views on the meeting. The first critiqued the association (of which he was a member), saying that associations were wrong to oppose this type of good nonprofit work and that such opposition was playing to stereotypes of the homeless. The second gave a more mixed approach. She asserted that nonprofits for the homeless were underfunded and did not always provide adequate services to the homeless population. The problem with a larger facility, in her view, was that it made it less likely that the nonprofit could support all the new tenants, thus creating spillover problems for the rest of the neighborhood. Besides, she said, the association had no legal way to stop the facility from opening. All they could do was use the parking issue to limit the total number of beds. In her view, the neighborhood association was not saying "Not in my backyard," it was saying "Please respect my backyard" by not building a facility that had more beds than a small nonprofit could support.

This is, in many ways, the crux of the justice issue in neighborhood associations. Neighborhoods are the site of structural (Friedman 1969) and systemic (Feagin 2014) racism, the site of what Bonilla-Silva (2010) calls a racist color-blind ideology that claims that welfare and culture undermine communities (without actually saying that such arguments are about race), and yet neighborhoods are also the site of powerful organizing campaigns to fight these very forces and ideologies. Thus we must ask, are micro-local concerns, such as worrying about parking spots and potholes, really cover for a wider segregative agenda? Is "There are no parking spots in our neighborhood" the easiest way to say "We don't want you to live here"? Or, does a focus on local infrastructure and quality of life actually lead to unjust and segregative outcomes even if that is not the intent? Does it disempower renters? This is not where the NIMBYism discussion starts, but in urban communities, it is where it ends. Can an association engaging in NIMBYism truly fight for justice?

To understand the NIMBY critique and the flaws of its universal application to neighborhood associations, it is necessary to go back and seek to understand NIMBYism itself. Hazardous waste disposal sites offer classic cases of NIMBYism (see Heiman 1990; Rabe 1994). It is generally understood that such disposal is a necessary evil, but no community wants these facilities in their neighborhood. Communities fight against hazardous waste disposal, knowing full well that it must be located somewhere and they just want it located somewhere other than in their neighborhood. Typically, such opposition is framed as selfish; communities are willing to fight something coming to them, knowing full well it will go to others. Heiman (1990) argues for a movement that will go beyond the politics of *not in my backyard* to a politics of *not in anyone's backyard*, but the connotations of selfish communities remain.

NIMBYism is a particularly powerful concept in urban communities, where it often takes on a racial or an anti-development tint – neighborhoods opposed to people or development are seen as not good for the neighborhood. Such urban situations can be quite diverse. Sometimes they involve local neighborhood activists who oppose development in a neighborhood for quality of life purposes. Sometimes they involve opposition to development because of fear of gentrification. Still other times, NIMBYism gets especially ugly. It becomes about not wanting certain types of people "in my backyard." Often, this is expressed in terms of being fearful of Section 8 renters who participate in the federal Section 8 housing voucher program. That fear can be a proxy for concerns about black families or other families of color moving into a community. Such NIMBY organizations and activists are scorned under two dominant narratives. Neighborhoods that oppose development or gentrification are opposing progress. Neighborhoods that oppose renters or low-income housing are bigoted.

In this way, NIMBYism is a clumsy, but necessary, umbrella for a wider pair of neighborhood inclinations. The first is engagement with development in ensure that it is positive for the long-term health of residents. The second is the concern (or fear) that certain groups of people might undermine the neighborhood. At times, such as in Faubourg St Johns, these two neighborhood approaches clearly overlap. The opposition to the new transitional housing for the homeless was, on its face, about neighborhood quality of life. There were concerns about parking spots. But the wider concern was about the "who" of the development, not the development itself. Most neighborhoods are pleased to see a vacant building activated in their neighborhood. That "who" is hidden in the haze of neighborhood associations. Is it fear of the individual people? Of housing values dropping? It is difficult to know because, as in the larger society, there is little explicit or frank discussion. It is easier to take a technocratic route and oppose the new development on the grounds that it does not meet the parking requirements, particularly because such racially neutral explanations fit society's requirement for color-blind public statements (Bonilla-Silva 2010).

The tension between these two values is implicit in many of the neighborhood choices and ideals throughout this book. Broadmoor was able to attract an Apex Youth Center, a community center, in part because other neighborhoods feared it might attract the "wrong kids" to the community. The Algiers Point Association became involved with local community police tactics because of fears that the "wrong" people might cross by ferry and commit crimes in the neighborhood. French Quarter Citizens Inc. focuses on quality of life enforcement, which targets businesses with practices they do not want in their communities. NIMBYism is an essential characteristic of a protective neighborhood association – saying "no" to development is a standard interpretation of protection. And yet, there seems to be a difference between opposing a restaurant seeking a liquor license, which residents worry might bring violence to a neighborhood, or a Take 5 Oil on a corner where residents would prefer a more resident-friendly establishment, and opposing low-income housing, which might bring the "wrong" people.

In New Orleans, associations did all of this. They opposed development because of the physical impact it might have on the neighborhood, and they opposed development because of the ways in which it might change the demographics of the neighborhood. This is particularly important for our understanding of the neighborhood movement and its embrace of elements of the right to the city. Such opposition and NIMBYism are closely linked to Harvey's (2012) argument that the right to the city is powerful in part because it empowers those without enough capital to buy commercial property to have a role in deciding what happens with urban spaces. In short, the power of residents to recapture control over urban space may be the same power that enables discrimination.

The idea that neighborhoods need protection *from* development deserves a longer discussion. For many neighborhoods, it is counterintuitive – we need development in order to have the type of quality of life and job opportunities necessary in a community. For a neighborhood such as Pilotland, which lacks basic neighborhood commercial entities like a pharmacy, development is wanted and encouraged as an antidote to historical disinvestment. But other neighborhoods are skeptical of development and particularly worried that unchecked development will in some way damage local residential communities. In the French Quarter, this skepticism manifests itself as opposition to Disneyfication (Harvey 2012), while in other neighborhoods the opposition has far less to do with the threat of tourism and more to do with the manner in which developers and companies can mistreat residential neighbors. These tensions played out in a development at the corner of Claiborne and Carrollton. The corner, one of the last undeveloped lots in the community, was within the Northwest Carrollton Neighborhood Association's boundaries, but it directly adjoined the Fontainebleau neighborhood.

For the Fontainebleau Improvement Association, that plot of land was critical to ensure the ideal lifestyle the neighborhood envisioned for itself. Years before, an iconic K&B grocery store had been on the lot. When K&B left, members of the association began taking steps to recruit a new grocery store to the community. For a neighborhood within walking distance of a university and boutique shopping, as well as of beautiful houses and a trolley line to the French Quarter, a grocery store was the final piece of the picturesque neighborhood puzzle. When Walgreens bought the block, local residents worried that there would be a second pharmacy rather than a grocery store. But Walgreens chose not to build on the lot for close to a decade. The neighborhood continued to try to recruit a grocery store, coming close to a deal with Wynn Dixie that fell through just prior to the storm. After Hurricane Katrina, as Walgreens prepared to build, the association finally had a stroke of luck. A member was writing insurance for a small local grocery store and sold it on opening another store on the Carrollton and Claiborne lot. The association remained involved as a key member of the neighborhood design committee, and the grocery store, called Robert's, created an imaginative, neighborhood-friendly urban layout for it. Residents called the association the spark that brought a grocery store to the community, even mentioning that attempts to recruit that grocery store had started before the neighborhood association across the street had even formed.

Members of the Northwest Carrollton Neighborhood Association remember the process differently. The association was extremely skeptical of Walgreens, citing the history of pharmacies buying and using properties as chess pieces in a battle over market share in the city. Pharmacies would buy corner lots that were ideal for development, not to develop them, but to protect their investment in nearby communities. If one pharmacy owned a site, it could prevent a competitor from building on the site and thus maintain a de facto monopoly for its nearby store.

When Walgreens delayed building on the Northwest Carrollton plot, it confirmed much of its local reputation. For the Northwest Carrollton neighborhood, the lack of development at its major commercial intersection was devastating. Houses adjacent to the blighted lot were abandoned. The abandoned site and the abandoned houses were an eyesore and a drag on the value of homes in the surrounding neighborhood. They were also a missed opportunity. Northwest Carrollton neighbors were proud of their community, a diverse population in an affordable, yet historical, neighborhood. The plot had the potential to further those values by bringing in local commercial activity that reaffirmed the neighborhood's character as a local, urban gem in a city of culture.

Walgreens was none of those things. In the words of the NCNA president, Kristen, it was "wrong to think that the solution to New Orleans recovery was an insulting Walgreens stamp." Worse still, the plot included large swathes of parking space. "It was Metarie. It was suburbia. It wasn't the reason New Orleanians came back." For neighbors, the plans for the development were worse still. The buildings faced the intersection of Claiborne and Carrollton Streets, while the backs of the two buildings faced the local neighborhood. The original plans not only failed to include an entrance for residents, who would have to walk nearly two blocks around the buildings just to enter them, but to add insult to injury, the plans included dumpsters along the back of the buildings that would face local houses, potentially dampening their value and ensuring that residents would awake to the sight and smell of garbage. The combination of a suburban-style plot with large expanses of parking, the utter disregard for the neighborhood in the design, and the lack of a nod to the history of architecture in the neighborhood, all confirmed to residents that Walgreens did not have the neighborhood's best interest in mind.

What followed was a fight that divided developers, politicians, and neighborhoods. Residents of Fontainebleau were thrilled to have a grocery store coming into a lot that they had feared would only have a pharmacy. They saw the development as an unqualified good, one that they had worked towards for years. Of course, the development also faced their neighborhood, inviting them in. For the Northwest Carrollton Neighborhood Association (NCNA), the development was seen as a significant threat to the neighborhood and could lead to its exclusion from its most prominent commercial development. The struggle escalated. The NCNA, feeling left out of negotiations, conducted what Kristen called "guerrilla warfare" to ensure they were heard. That included hanging sheets from existing buildings on the site and painting "Walgreens Kills Neighborhoods" on them. The issue became so controversial that a candidate for city council, Shelly Midura, launched her campaign at the site of the grocery store, backing the Northwest Carrollton Neighborhood Association.

The battle between the neighborhoods ended with modest changes to the plan. The two neighborhoods hoped that the buildings would reflect the historical architecture in the community. One concession was Walgreens, whose building included turrets mimicking the historical architecture at the nearby Chicle Gum Factory, which had been on the National Register for Historic Places and later was refurbished as the headquarters of a construction company. That factory had long been a neighborhood icon. The Robert's grocery store also moved to a more urban setting, with a compact site that did not present such a large back facade to the Northwest Carrollton neighborhood. Kristen called the new design, and the grocery store's success after opening, a sign that communities can work together with developers to create viable commercial projects without damaging communities or profits. The final design even changed the orientation of the building, making it easier for residents to enter and exit the complex.

The Walgreens and Robert's development, and the conflict it engendered across the Northwest Carrollton Neighborhood Association and the Fontainebleau Improvement Association is a Rorschach test of the New Orleans neighborhood movement and its interpretation of the right to the city. This example shows how giving city residents control over development might actually play out, and it confirms the skepticism of Purcell (2006, 1922) and his "local trap." Here, the local trap lies in assuming that a process that empowers neighborhoods would result in a democratically just development. The Walgreens development shows how complex achieving that end can be. Empowering neighborhood associations by necessity often means empowering communities with more influence. Developers and businesses can *choose* the neighborhoods with which they choose to align, empowering communities that face fewer risks from development than those who face greater risks (i.e., the rear facade and the dumpsters). The Walgreens development is also an example of how powerful what Louise calls "developer's logic" can be. Neighborhood associations are often in favor of development because it means converting an empty lot into commercial real estate. It can help the neighborhood and help provide jobs, but other neighborhoods worry that the market itself will not protect residents. The NCNA conflict had multiple players and was a continuation of the quality of life focus of neighborhood associations. There is a concern with how development will affect things such as driving, parking, home values, and other local concerns. This concern conflicts with a broader idea that some development is better than blight and empty lots. Residents, too, express concern that the market, at any given moment, may produce a short-term solution that is an improvement but misses the long-term opportunity afforded a neighborhood. NIMBYism against development in urban neighborhoods is a cocktail of different interests, from quality of life, to long-term character of the neighborhood, to a preference for walkable, new, urbanist design.

Those struggles played out over and over again, both in New Orleans, and in the specific neighborhoods of Fontainebleau and

Northwest Carrollton more than once. Those communities faced a similar struggle over a Take 5 Oil development on another lot. The business was largely focused on commuters using the main thoroughfares running through the community. The president of the Fontainebleau Improvement Association insisted that he too would rather have a coffee shop or a bookshop at the lot, but, he argued, the lot had been empty for ages and some economic development was better than none. But those who opposed Take 5 Oil argued that it might be better to hold out, particularly as the neighborhood grew, for better commercial development. Over time, gas stations and oil change facilities will not change a neighborhood in the way that small, resident-friendly commercial shops will. Take 5 Oil may only be an optimal solution in the short-term, but neighborhood associations do protect the long-term interests of a neighborhood.

In these ways, neighborhood associations are fighting for justice and upholding the right to the city. Their NIMBYism is directed towards ensuring that neighborhoods are not railroaded by development that ignores them, preferring to appeal to more lucrative commuters who drive through their neighborhoods or to tourists who come for a short visit. And NIMBY-inclined neighborhood activists also try to protect the long-term interests of the community by holding out for development that improves the residents' quality of life, strengthening the neighborhood. But existing racial geography and history play into such debates. Legacies of disinvestment in black communities often make such communities more interested in attracting any development, even chains that might be looked down upon by more affluent neighbors.

For example, the Northwest Carrollton Neighborhood Association opposed a grocery store and a pharmacy, facilities that low-income neighborhoods such as Pilotland desperately want in their communities. Even residents of the privileged Fontainebleau neighborhood expressed frustration that, without Robert's, their community was a food desert. These facilities are critical to a community. Neighborhood activists argue that they lack the power to fully stop projects, and thus they are just negotiating aggressively to ensure that development is resident-friendly (their negotiation tactics are examined more fully in Chapter 6), but these NIMBY tactics run the real risk of throwing the baby out with the bathwater. Indeed, a "Yes in my backyard" (YIMBY) movement has sprouted in response to NIMBY tactics that are seen as delaying good development (Ramos 2016).

A decade before Katrina, Faubourg Lafayette went through a similar controversy. Just as in Northwest Carrollton, the neighborhood was a food desert without a grocery store. Located in Central City, a historically African-American neighborhood in one of the most crime-ridden areas of New Orleans, the Historic Faubourg Lafayette Association opposed the proposed development of a grocery store in 1998 on a couple of grounds. (1) The sprawling suburban model of development featured a large store and expansive parking lots, inappropriate for an urban setting; and (2) the development designs called for the demolition of eight historical homes. The similarities with Northwest Carrollton are indicative of the wider dynamics between development and neighborhood associations. In both of these neighborhoods, associations opposed a proposed development because of its physical impact on their neighborhood. In Northwest Carrollton, the association worried that the design of the development would negatively impact existing houses. In Faubourg Lafayette, the conflict was over existing historical homes that were to be demolished for the grocery store. In both locations, the expansive parking lots were seen as a suburban model of development unfit for an urban neighborhood.

In Faubourg Lafayette, the development never got off the ground (in part because of the association's aggressive campaign – detailed in Chapter 6). The result puts the limitations of the emphasis on neighborhood protection under the spotlight. In Faubourg Lafayette, the association helped to protect historical homes, but the central lot remained vacant. It was only years later that the empty lot became apartments, developed by a faith-based nonprofit focused on affordable housing. The neighborhood remained without a grocery store. In this case, the neighborhood preference for protection came into direct conflict with other priorities, such as economic development and even food justice.

The conflict between values plays out not only in big-ticket development, but in smaller development decisions. In New Orleans, the preference to protect neighborhood infrastructure and residential quality of life often conflicts with economic development. Other times, it conflicts with the city's rich culture of entertainment. Those conflicts are particularly stark in neighborhoods such as the French Quarter, where Disneyfication and the constant pressures of tourism intersect with cultural gems such as live performance venues. Short-term rentals were a key issue for French Quarter Citizens Inc. and the Vieux Carré

Property Owners, Residents, and Associates. The battle over short-term rentals is, in part, one of residential quality of life. Louise, the executive director of VCPORA, struggles with properties purchased exclusively to put on AirBnB, a website promoting short-term rentals. These properties, often situated in the middle of a residential neighborhood, can have extremely disruptive inhabitants. Rather than having a long-term neighbor, residents are beset with a never-ending onslaught of bachelor parties, late-night parties, and drunken visitors that do not think twice before urinating in bushes outside. Owners of such properties have little incentive to crack down on guests, as it might lead to poor reviews, meaning neighborhood residents are left to convince guests to be less disruptive.

Short-term rentals bring to light broader justice issues for members of neighborhood associations. Short-term rentals compete with local hotels and facilities that are more highly regulated. Some local neighborhood activists, such as the president of French Quarter Citizens Inc., own local facilities that suffer negative economic consequences from an under-regulated short-term rental market that does not meet the same health and safety requirements as hotels. As with much of the "sharing economy," part of the struggle is over the appropriate role of government in regulating these services. The ride-sharing company Uber faces similar questions. While the service is popular, it shows the ways in which an unregulated industry will almost inevitably pass on costs and risks to its employees. Thus, short-term rentals and AirBnB are part of a wider question of regulation and of how to treat employees in the sharing economy. For neighborhoods, perhaps the greatest impact of the proliferation of properties bought specifically as vessels for full-time, short-term rentals is that it takes properties off the long-term rental market. After Hurricane Katrina, rents shot up for New Orleans residents. Now, additional units are coming off the market and many are converted to short-term rentals. Once again rents are rising.

Affordable housing is a critical justice issue. Here, the neighborhood protection ideal intersects with Harvey's (2012) concept of Disneyfication. The core of Disneyfication is that it prioritizes tourism, and the economic development tied to it, at the expense of a living, vibrant neighborhood. The right to the city is supposed to be a locally based movement to counterbalance the economic pressures that tourism puts on a community. In many ways, this is how the short-term rental controversy in New Orleans is playing out. The economic influence of tourism is leading to an influx of investors buying homes for the explicit purpose of renting them out to tourists. Local neighborhood associations, and their fight to regulate short-term rentals, show that neighborhood associations can play a role as protector of resident interests. But the short-term rental debate also shows how that conflict, between economic interests and resident interests, can overlap with other justice issues in unpredictable ways. In this case, the struggle against short-term rentals is a struggle for justice in rent prices and affordable housing. But neighborhood associations can just as easily cut the other way in that debate; the Coliseum Square Neighborhood Association explicitly fought scatter-site affordable housing in its neighborhood. As we will see later in this chapter, renters are not always welcomed by associations. Sometimes they are even seen as something from which neighborhoods need protection. This is critical, because it provides a second layer to the monolithic struggle of development – neighborhood associations may be a counterpoint against development while *simultaneously* using their powers to discriminate against potential residents. The conflict between resident rights and economic development is not just one of neoliberalism, it spills into other realms in unpredictable ways. Sometimes the priorities of associations further the cause of affordable housing, and sometimes NIMBYism is the bane of affordable housing.

The short-term rental struggle in New Orleans demonstrates this in yet another way. It shows how that struggle over residential quality of life can come into conflict with a city's rich cultural heritage. The short-term rental debate is not solely about properties bought for the express purpose of short-term rentals. Sites such as AirBnB have also made the long-time practice of renting out rooms in one's own home during Mardi Gras and Jazz Fest infinitely easier. In New Orleans, many of my friends chose to leave the city during high tourist season. For those on a tight budget, renting out their home was a way to recoup funds. For renters, the two weekends of Jazz Fest could sometimes fund two or three months' rent. This has long been part of the cultural fabric of living in New Orleans, a way for everyday residents to capitalize on the demand for tourism. For those who have rented out their homes for decades and for whom it is an important part of their cash flow, the complaints against AirBnB ring hollow because they also see it as taking away a cultural practice that they have taken advantage of for years. And AirBnB advocates have conflated these issues, using sympathy for the cultural practice to garner support for year-round rentals. This distinction was eventually enshrined into law; short-term rentals were banned in the French Quarter but required licensing elsewhere in the city for a maximum number of nights rented each year. This was an attempt to support family-style renting while limiting the purchase of properties solely to be listed on AirBnB.

The cultural conflict with neighborhood quality of life played out in other ways as well. Ulysses, the president of French Quarter Citizens Inc., was successful in advocating noise legislation to protect residents. These noise restrictions applied not only to bars blasting canned music out of windows, but also to live music – an integral and beloved aspect of the city's cultural heritage. That meant that technically the French Quarter's tradition of buskers was in peril, something that riled up both musicians and long-standing supporters of the New Orleans musical culture.

That conflict came to a head over the To Be Continued (TBC) Brass Band. The New Orleans brass band tradition, featuring a trumpet, trombone, saxophone, tuba, snare drum, and bass drum, is a unique feature of the musical heritage of New Orleans. These bands developed a brand of hip-hop-influenced jazz while walking in parades. The TBC Brass Band gathered at the corner of Canal Street and Bourbon Street each night to play for hours. For many tourists, it was their first introduction to New Orleans culture, and in the opinion of many residents, it was a much-needed infusion of culture to a Bourbon Street scene that reveled in clichéd debauchery. For some French Quarter residents, however, it was a disaster. The brass band could be heard throughout the French Quarter for hours, often past midnight, keeping children and the elderly awake. It clearly violated noise restrictions, but when the police tried to clear the band, New Orleans residents came to its defense. The lines became stark, with neighborhood associations arguing that maintaining quality of life for residents was critical to the future of the Quarter and cultural watchdogs claiming that people who moved into the Quarter knew about live-music traditions and had no right to limit the bands. Neighborhood associations thus found themselves on the opposite side of a culture battle. So many times, they had used character of place to support the neighborhood. Now they were hearing the same arguments in support of the band. The same battle was playing out throughout the city. Bars such as Mimi's, in Faubourg Marigny, and Bacchanals, in Bywater (see Hancock 2011), occasionally were forced to stop the live music they had been playing for years because they had never sought the correct licensing for live music, and neighborhood activists had found out. Thus, the right to the city manifests itself in unexpected ways. The neighborhood protection ethic comes into direct conflict with the city's broader embrace of its cultural heritage, a conflict made doubly intense by the racial implications of a Bourbon Street tourism scene that culturally appropriates jazz and black culture. Harvey (2012) writes about how development can undermine a city's unique cultural heritage. Development in cities such as Barcelona merges with standard waterfront development in other metropolitan cities. But neighborhood politics can also be an oppositional force in conflict with a city's cultural ideals. NIMBYism can just as easily oppose live local music as it can oppose suburban sprawl.

NIMBYism is, in many ways, a manifestation of the way the New Orleans neighborhood movement embraces elements of the right to the city. It is the triumph of the parochial, the neighborhood activity that Leontidou (2010) argues does not quite meet the requirements of a movement because of its link to a specific geographical location. The geographic boundedness of neighborhood associations and the neighborhood protection ideal embraced by them can both empower residents to oppose Disneyfication and enable neighborhoods to undercut cultural heritage. It is not a catch-all solution to urban politics, but another perspective in a wide negotiation of priorities. Neighborhood protection can be a set piece in a struggle against development, but it can just as easily be a set piece in a struggle against a beloved local music venue. And, at its most complicated, the neighborhood protection ideal can be a set piece designed to exclude people from a community.

Just as the ideal of neighborhood protection can come into conflict with economic development and a city's cultural heritage, neighborhood protection can come into conflict with specific groups of people. Protecting the neighborhood could mean limiting the extent to which it is overrun with student housing from surrounding universities; it could mean zoning that makes the neighborhood more expensive for both homebuyers and renters, and it could mean opposing affordable housing. These types of NIMBYism, focused specifically on cohorts of people, come with a second risk, that the neighborhood protection ideal may be a color-blind way of speaking that hides racial discrimination or discrimination against other vulnerable groups (see Bonilla-Silva 2010). The history of neighborhood protection and quality of life has long served as an intermediary for racial discrimination, allowing neighborhood residents to claim that the issue is not *really* race, it is the good of the neighborhood, all while actively discriminating. This was famously the case with the busing issue when schools were desegregated in the 1970s and 1980s. Delmont (2016) argues that the focus on busing allowed white families to argue that they opposed desegregation without explaining the obvious: that they did not want their children to go to school with *those* kids. Instead, parents could talk about the impact of busing on their communities and neighborhoods. Delmont (2016) argues that these issues, and the focus on busing in particular, are codes that allowed neighbors to exert racial preference without the stigma of racialized discourse and that were enabled by a media that was more sympathetic to white inconvenience than black civil rights.

Many of the same issues play out in neighborhoods in New Orleans, so much so that NIMBYism is a Rorschach test of types. Are such neighborhood protection ideals actually a Trojan horse for racial discrimination? Are the ideals themselves racially problematic? How legitimate are those ideals in neighborhoods? But these may be the wrong questions. Regardless of the intent of such neighborhood ideals, they have racial *impacts*. This is the heart of both structural (Friedman 1969) and systemic racism (Feagin 2014). Racism need not manifest as individual discrimination or animosity (Bonilla-Silva 2010). It may manifest as a preference for neighborhood continuity or skepticism of renters. There is a long history of housing and the community values that have contributed, both explicitly and implicitly, to segregation (Ladson-Billings and Tate 1995).

I argue that neighborhood activists find themselves working across this spectrum. Some explicitly use neighborhood protectionism to hide racial preferences. Others are unaware of implicit biases that are hidden by their neighborhood defense. And still others wrestle with the racial implications of their choices, deciding either to ignore the neighborhood ideal so as to avoid negative racial outcomes or to embrace neighborhood protection despite racial consequences. In other words, just as neighborhood protection comes into conflict with economic development and cultural heritage, it comes into conflict with racial justice, and neighborhood activists make decisions across the spectrum.

It is a mistake to conflate conflict around busing directly with NIMBYism in urban neighborhoods. As Delmont (2016) details, busing was almost entirely a proxy for desegregation. With a segregated school system, white (and black) parents already had busing in their communities. So, it almost certainly was not the case that busing was the actual issue that concerned parents. Parents were concerned with desegregation. In that case, the neighborhood protection ideal was almost entirely used to hide real preferences. Many of the cases we have already discussed, such as the NCNA's opposition to Walgreens, have little explicit racial connotation. In these cases, neighborhood protectionism is a core philosophy that is genuinely being pursued (even at the expense of development). That also happens when NIMBYism extends beyond *We do not want that development* in our neighborhood to *We do not want those people* in our neighborhood. For example, in Upper Audubon, prior to Hurricane Katrina, the association fiercely opposed a student housing development by Tulane University. This is common in many cities throughout the United States and beyond as local neighborhoods feel pressure from local universities. Sometimes this comes in the form of increased cost of living or gentrification. But these were not the worries in Upper Audubon, where the association quite explicitly focused on increasing property values. In Upper Audubon, students were seen as bad neighbors. They were loud, threw late parties, did not put out their trash at the right times, and, as temporary members of the neighborhood, were not involved in local civic life. The Upper Audubon preferred steady homeowners to a revolving door of twenty-one-year-olds as next-door neighbors. This quite clearly meets the criteria of NIMBYism – the neighborhood is not denying that student housing is necessary, but fighting it because it is an inconvenience in their neighborhood. And yet, it almost certainly is an inconvenience, as anyone who has lived next to (or in) student housing can attest. Here, Heiman's (1990) argument for a movement from *not in my backyard* to *not in anyone's backyard* makes little sense. Upper Audubon is attractive as a neighborhood in part because of its proximity to the university. The neighbors want the good (jobs, property values, vibrant commercial corridor) without the negative (student housing) and will fight to keep student housing out of Upper Audubon even if it means other neighborhoods will have more of it. This is a critical, largely unexamined downside to how neighborhood movements operationalize the right to the city. A right to the city that prioritizes neighborhoods and residents almost inevitably puts them in conflict with one another. Allowing residents more influence over development opens doors for protecting slums or affordable housing – as is seen in Brazil and Mexico – but it also opens the door for NIMBYism and neighborhood competition. The vast majority of neighborhood associations embrace neighborhood protectionism, which often results in a conflict over prioritizing affordable housing and vulnerable populations. This is foreseen in the right to the city theory. Theorists such as Marcuse (2009), Harvey (2012), and Purcell (2002) argue that the mantle of the right to the city can be taken by groups with other priorities. That is exactly how the right to the city played out in New Orleans, and the evaluation of these activities depends on the prioritization and balancing of these multiple value systems.

As such, neighborhood protection becomes a test of both intentions and the ways that discrimination is both structural and systemic. Was the Upper Audubon Association right to oppose student housing in its neighborhood? There is almost no way to judge, unless there is a wider framework that balances the wider needs of the community with the specific costs to individual residents. And just as a democratic analysis of associations shows them to engage in a politics of last resort, many neighborhood activists see their own protectionism as a last line of defense against systems that impact them unfairly. We know from research on color-blindness (Bonilla-Silva 2010) and from Alexander's *The New Jim Crow* (2010) that neutral intentions can still be damaging and that whiteness can be an asset in these communities, as politicians seeking to redevelop neighborhoods see white families as a source of capital. The history of housing makes such matters even more complex; neighborhood protectionism is mediated by a history of racial discrimination even when it is used to fight against such discrimination.

For example, in Faubourg Lafayette (over a decade after the fight over the impact a grocery store development would have on historical homes in the neighborhood) a handful of young, white parents bought homes in the neighborhood. While most New Orleanians looked at Faubourg Lafayette and saw it placed square in the middle of Central City, an area of the city with a sometimes ugly reputation for crime and disinvestment, these new homeowners saw an opportunity. The neighborhood was just across Route 90 from the Central Business District, and a short walk or bike ride from the French Quarter. Further, the neighborhood was one of the few not to flood during Hurricane Katrina, and housing prices were extraordinarily low.

Becky was a mother in one of the few new, young, white families that moved into the neighborhood. She discovered it through Felicity Street Redevelopment, a tiny nonprofit that buys houses, revamps them, then sells them. Becky was effusive in her praise of the neighborhood, and lost no opportunity to recruit new residents. She will walk potential recruits through the process to purchase a property inexpensively at a Sheriff's sale and lay out the minimum expenses for the home to be livable.

Becky's excitement over the neighborhood was contagious, only waning when she began to speak of the origins of the Faubourg Lafayette Neighborhood Association. The association had recently been created, though some long-time neighbors considered it a revival of the Historic Faubourg Lafayette Neighborhood Association that had folded years before – the same association that had fought to preserve historical homes from the grocery store development. However, Becky struggled with an organization on her street called the Mission, a homeless shelter that took advantage of the neighborhood's close proximity to the raised I-10 Highway. Many of the homeless use the I-10 as a shield from the relentless New Orleans sun, so having a shelter in proximity made a lot of sense.

From the perspective of the shelter and the city, the Mission was an ideal band-aid to a serious problem. Its location made it perfect for reaching out and helping the homeless community. Becky did not share their enthusiasm, as she had to live with the consequences of the shelter. Every morning, she would arise at 6 a.m., just after the homeless were let out of the shelter. Homeless people walked through her yard, occasionally urinating on her house, often tossing used beer cans or worse into the yard. And so, before she could let her young children out to play, she had to go out and clean up the needles and cans from her lawn. When she went to her city council representative, Stacey Head, about the issue, she was told to form a neighborhood association so she would have more clout.

In many ways, Becky's story is a critical test for our understanding of neighborhood associations and the neighborhood protection ideal. This is the touching account of a mother who tried to improve her neighborhood. But it also presents the acceptable face of a NIMBY effort. Her daily life gives insight into the motivations of such neighborhood protectionism. It is easy to feel compassion for a mother who daily has to clean up her yard before she can let her children outside. And yet opposition to the Mission is a genuine justice issue, for it actively disenfranchises and hurts the homeless population who lack the cachet of being a young, white mother new to a neighborhood in need of new homeowners.

The same dynamic emerges in other neighborhoods struggling to maintain their neighborhood quality of life. In Sugar Hill, the neighborhood association built a fantastic relationship with Dillard University. The historically black university is located just up the street, and after the storm it formed a community development corporation to help with the storm recovery. The university played a role in bringing health clinics to the area, working with twelve to fifteen associations after the storm to create their own plans and find their own resources. It was one of the Sugar Hill Neighborhood Association's closest allies. But the university also received a donation of two properties in the Sugar Hill neighborhood. As long as the properties were being used for faculty and administration housing, there was no controversy, but Dillard repurposed one of them for an environmental remediation program that placed non-violent first-time ex-convicts at the property.

It took only one or two alleged incidents involving grown men supposedly catcalling after underaged girls walking home from school for the neighborhood association to grow impatient. It finally responded by opposing a land-use change the university needed for other properties. This opposition was leveraged to remove the first-time offender program from the neighborhood. The head of the Dillard Community Development Corporation (CDC) said that "no one wins in things like this," but the entire incident served as a reminder that relationships are multi-faceted. Tammy and her association had no qualms about working with the Dillard CDC on projects while aggressively opposing a land-use measure to ensure their voice was heard when the CDC overstepped what the neighborhood viewed as its boundaries.

The Dreux Avenue Good Neighbors Society faced a similar challenge. A small block within the Gentilly Terrace and Garden Neighborhood association boundaries had mixed-use zoning that attracted a variety of artists, who could use the ground floor for a studio and live upstairs. One of those artists was Erin, who would later found the Dreux Avenue Good Neighbors Society. She loved her new neighborhood, until a crusty local neighbor passed away. That neighbor had been living in a six-plex apartment by himself, and when a developer bought the property and turned it into apartments, neighbors noticed changes. Erin's immediate reaction to the new apartments was, "Six new neighbors!" But the residents in the close-knit block became wary of the new neighbors' loitering and drinking on the lawn throughout the day. There were almost two dozen calls to the police about the six-plex over a span of six months. Rumors also spread about the renters. Matt, a founding member of the Dreux Avenue Good Neighbor Society who lived next door to the six-plex, called it "literally a loony-bin without a gatekeeper." He was convinced that the apartments were being used as some kind of mental health facility, insisting that "the people were actually, literally, by definition, crazy." The developer denied this vigorously to Matt and to others. Matt put the big question this way: "People that lived in a mental facility and have criminal records, can they just show up in my neighborhood? The answer is yes."

It was a question that some of the residents of the block struggled with together. The block was diverse, both in terms of races and professions. The neighbors saw themselves as open-minded. They did not see themselves as typical not-in-my-backyard reactionaries. Matt's biggest complaint was that his new neighbors were plopped down into a new neighborhood with no support. Erin went to the local neighborhood organization, Gentilly Terrace and Gardens Neighborhood Association, but found the problem was confined to a single block and did not rise high on the larger association's radar. She went to her local council member. Same result. Erin put her house up for sale because she no longer felt safe. When her neighbors found out, they were devastated. The block bound together and started the Dreux Avenue Good Neighbors Society. The joke was right there in the title – all they wanted was "good neighbors" like the ones they had had before their recent problems.

The issues that concern Dreux Avenue and Faubourg Lafayette are typical of neighborhood associations, but they also show the danger that NIMBYism can lead to when it intersects with race. Issues such as increased phone calls to the police, loitering, and other "suspicious activities" intersect with research that indicate that African-Americans are more likely to face discipline in schools. Similarly, the #BlackLivesMatter movement has heightened the national consciousness regarding negative reactions to African-Americans by police and other communities. Systemic racism theorizes that these communities are more likely to be seen as threats, and thus experience more aggressive enforcement. In other words, in a city where politics and poverty are racialized, and in a culture where policing is racialized, the prospect that NIMBYism is a code for race is a frightening but inevitable one.

The post-Katrina landscape was largely interpreted by both researchers and politicians through a racial lens. Race and loss were tied together in New Orleans long before Hurricane Katrina. In New Orleans, race permeates politics, history, development, and culture. Immediately after the hurricane, it was racialized through the images of looting, rape, and murder that dominated the media (Tierney et al. 2006). A consensus emerged after the storm that the fractured history of discrimination embedded in development patterns meant that African-American residents had the most difficult recovery (Hartman and Squires 2006). African-American families saw their homes hit the hardest by flooding, largely because they lived in the most at-risk areas. Hartman and Squires (ibid.) argue that, in this sense, Hurricane Katrina was not a *natural* disaster, it was a *man-made* one. It also reflected how segregation and discrimination regarding property rights sits at the center of understanding racial justice (Ladson-Billings and Tate 1995). The same racial influences affected the lives of many after the storm. Race was embedded in the preference given to homeowners over renters and the efforts to change public housing. It was embedded in the politics of gentrification and recovery.

Low-lying lands, with the highest flood risk, were historically African-American and low income.[1] As flood protection improved, population in these areas increased. This had a counterintuitive effect; the better the flood protection, the worse the eventual disaster that overwhelmed that protection (Kates et al. 2006). Fussell et al. (2010) demonstrate the effects of such policy after Hurricane Katrina. Fewer African-Americans returned to the city, but this racial difference was largely, though not completely, explained by the greater damage inflicted on their houses. A notable exception was the decision to demolish public housing despite the fact that the units had suffered little storm damage; this decision disproportionately affected African-Americans, who were the majority of tenants in public housing.

The legacy of unequal development played itself out during the storm. It also played itself out in state policy after the storm. The state-run Road Home program was privatized (Adams 2013) and it focused exclusively on homeowners. The policy had serious problems for that constituency; it was based, for example, on reimbursements that were often late in coming. There was a similar problem with insurance policies; homeowners have scars from battles with insurance companies and government over what they would be paid after the storm. Yet, for renters, the policy agenda was an even greater debacle. Housing stock was decimated after the storm. Limited availability of housing caused rents to soar. There was no aid program for low-income renters facing the compounded financial problems of loss of personal property, extended evacuation costs, and increased rent. Again, here the city's legacy of racialized housing policy had an immediate effect after the storm.

To make matters worse, the Lafitte public housing project was demolished despite having suffered only sixteen inches of flooding. Demolition took place three years after the storm, and rebuilding was delayed even longer. A squeeze on the low-income sector of the housing market resulted, and even greater number of families were searching for affordable housing within the city. African-Americans bore the brunt of these bad decisions and thus were skeptical of the political forces behind them. Some African-American leaders went as far as to accuse business leaders of trying to gentrify New Orleans and make it more difficult for blue-collar African-Americans to live there. In one sequence in his memoir (2011), Mayor Ray Nagin talks about a conflict with business owners over this very issue. He was meeting with business leaders in Houston, and in part because of pressure from his African-American constituency, he accused them of trying to keep African-Americans out of the recovering city. The business leaders denied any such intention, but suspicions remained. Politically, this seemed to be playing out. After Hurricane Katrina, the city council had a white majority for the first time in decades. Mayor Nagin, originally seen as a moderate supported by white businessmen who did well in majority white neighborhoods, embraced a strategy to reach out to the black population in his re-election campaign. On January 16, 2006, he gave an infamous speech, defending New Orleans as a chocolate city: "We, as black people, it's time. It's time for us to come together. It's time for us to rebuild a New Orleans – then that should be a chocolate New Orleans. And I don't care what people are saying uptown or wherever they are, this city will be chocolate at the end of the day. This city will be a majority African American city. It's the way God wants it to be." Ishiwata (2011) argues that the reaction to this speech exemplifies neoliberalism's ability to erase vulnerable people. Black leaders from other communities, such as film-maker Spike Lee, argued that they would not put it past white leaders to try to disperse black people in the aftermath of the storm. Ishiwata (2011) argues that conservative responses to the storm problematized black families as being at the core of the disaster. Simultaneously, media accounts highlighted the racial aspects of inequity in New Orleans, and post-Katrina President Bush's approval ratings with African-Americans plummeted. Racial justice became the dominant frame for understanding the reaction to the storm, a principle highlighted by accounts of shotgun blasts by whites at blacks seeking refuge in Algiers Point (Johnson 2011b) and by accounts that surrounding suburbs such as Gretna guarded their borders with barriers and authorities to keep New Orleans residents from entering their community. While some (Johnson 2011a, xxxvi) argue that "the racial justice argument is dull-edged" in favor of the neoliberalism lens, the dominant mode for understanding New Orleans after Hurricane Katrina was one of race.

As voting by blacks plummeted (Logan 2006), partially due to people's difficulties returning to the city, changes took on a racial hue. High-profile leaders, such as Chief Ronald Serpass of the New Orleans Police Department and eventually Mayor Mitch Landrieu, were white. The city council was majority white. Mayor Ray Nagin was re-elected, but his constituency almost entirely flipped; he went from winning largely white neighborhoods and being popular with the business elite to depending on winning largely black neighborhoods in his re-election campaign. The precision of racial politics was built on a complicated relationship with race in the city. New Orleans has a history of making sharp distinctions within its black population. Light-skinned descendants of French slaves in Tremé, the first free black neighborhood in New Orleans, were considered higher-class "Creoles." These families were central to black leadership emanating from New Orleans's 7th Ward (Hirsch and Logsdon 1992). In contrast, Dyson and Elliot (2010) write that "New Orleans invented the brown paper bag party – usually at a gathering in a home – where anyone darker than the bag attached to the door was denied entrance. The brown paper bag criterion survives as a metaphor for how the black cultural elite quite literally establishes a caste along color lines *within* black life." Darker-skinned blacks faced a challenging and a diverse array of discrimination.

In the city's oldest African-American–owned bookstore, a patron told me, "You are what's wrong with this city." It was an expression

I was to hear often, that as a young, white educator, I was soaking up recovery dollars that local residents could have used to get back on their feet. That criticism had resonance in light of the stunning number of African-American teachers who were fired after the storm. Local journalist Jed Horne (2008) described the city as having a "bohemian renaissance." Gentrification narratives played out in neighborhoods such as Faubourg Marigny and the Bywater. Some residents took to calling the Bywater "Little Portland" because of the presence of hipsters on one-gear bikes, the chicken farming in people's backyards, and the plethora of vegetarian restaurants that popped up in the communities. These communities had their own struggles. The Bywater was the location of a showdown between younger residents who wanted higher-density housing (leading to more nightlife and culture) and largely older residents, who favored a quieter neighborhood. The younger residents helped revive many of the city's cultural traditions. Local cultural institutions, such as the Candlelight Lounge in Tremé, saw an influx of younger, whiter patrons. The bar bought the building next door, knocked down the walls, and expanded. Second Lines, the famous parades that, before the storm, often served to commemorate community leaders who had passed away, were almost always held by black communities. Since then, they have become interracial.

Views on these developments are mixed. For some small businesses, the influx of new residents eager to participate in New Orleans's unique cultural heritage is a blessing, allowing traditions that might have faded from lack of capital to survive. But the influx of young, white residents also lit a fire under a vicious debate over cultural appropriation, "defined broadly as the use of a culture's symbols, artifacts, genres, rituals, or technologies by members of another culture" (Rogers 2006, 474). In particular, Mardi Gras Indians, whose costumes are synonymous with black culture in the city, were a flashpoint. Many within the Mardi Gras Indian tribes spent all year sewing costumes with elaborate feathers and sequins on cardboard, creating headdresses and full-body costumes. At the same time, photographers took pictures of the stunning costumes and sold them online. The capitalization of black traditions, with few blacks themselves taking part in the profits, led to resentment, and in the years after the storm, it was common to see Mardi Gras Indians with signs that told tourists not to take pictures of them without their permission.

Neighborhood associations, by virtue of being residential entities, largely avoided the appropriation debate. But associations faced a similarly tricky debate, with racial connotations, over the place of renters in the revitalized New Orleans. From the beginning, renters received little to no financial assistance. The state's Road Home program was perilously flawed (see Adams 2013). It privatized aid and was slow to reimburse homeowners, but it ignored renters *entirely*. Renters were forced to evacuate the city, lost many of their possessions, and lived out of pocket in the surrounding region for months before they could return to the city. When (and if) they did return, they faced a shortage of rentable units because of the extensive housing damage. With public housing demolished and rental housing in short supply, there was pressure (and need) for an expansion of affordable housing units. But neighborhood associations were largely skeptical of such developments, seeing renters and affordable housing units as threatening both housing prices and the neighborhood's character. To make matters more complex, in a city where race and socio-economics often overlap and in which blackness and poverty are too often conflated, claims about threats to the neighborhood too often became about the race of the people who moved in. It was like watching the nation's historical use of neighborhood and community character to further segregation's happening in real time.

These debates were not limited to white neighborhoods. Yes, white neighborhoods such as Coliseum Square fought to avoid the scatter-site housing surrounding public housing developments (see Adams 2013), but black neighborhoods faced pressure from renters and middle-class black neighborhoods could also be skeptical about affordable housing in their communities. Marzyeh, a board member of the Eastern New Orleans Neighborhood Advisory Council, lived in a typical New Orleans East dwelling. It was a stand-alone house in the midst of a beautiful, suburban-styled neighborhood. The dwelling reflected the allure of New Orleans East – to provide an opportunity for middle-class blacks to pursue the American dream of a house with a white picket fence. That dream was endangered, Marzheh claimed, by the high proportion of subsidized housing being built in her section of the city. She insisted that New Orleans East was home to 40 per cent of the city's total subsidized housing. At the same time, New Orleans East received what she called "unevenly, evenly applied" recovery dollars. She argued that dollars for recovery were being spread equally throughout the city, despite the fact that areas like New Orleans East were vulnerable, low-lying, and had significantly more damage thus a greater need for recovery dollars.

Spreading dollars equally hid inequity and disadvantage. Both of these claims had distinct racial undertones. Marzyeh pointed out that if funds were applied equally, areas with little to no flood damage got a share of the funds, while areas with massive flooding were left without enough resources. But because African-American families tend to live disproportionately in low-lying areas like New Orleans East or the Lower Ninth, they were systematically under-resourced. Even though Marzyeh bemoaned unequal funding, she also opposed increasing subsidized housing in New Orleans East. Marzyeh took care to explain that her opposition to additional subsidized housing was not a racial issue, but she was frank about how touchy the issue could be politically. Homeowners in New Orleans East expressed many of the same not-in-my-backyard fears often heard in other neighborhoods. They were wary of renters and people on subsidized housing because they believed those populations failed to keep the neighborhood clean and property values high. But in New Orleans East, this NIMBYism came with added baggage; it looked as though the middle-class black population was just as eager as the downtown white population to exclude poor blacks. When the black middle-class community did not oppose renters, they faced a disproportionate share of affordable housing as a result.

The skepticism of renters was a constant across virtually every neighborhood association, though not with every member within them. Neighborhood leaders from French Quarter Citizens Inc., the Historic Faubourg Lafayette Association, the Dreux Avenue Good Neighbors Society, the Irish Channel Neighborhood Association, the Sugar Hill Neighborhood Association, the Fontainebleau Improvement Association, the Pilotland Neighborhood Association, and the Lake Carmel Neighborhood Association each expressed skepticism that renters were good for a neighborhood. Sometimes the rhetoric was explicit and racial, but most often it sounded like the following quote from a board member of Felicity Street Redevelopment Inc., a non-profit that operated within the Historic Faubourg Lafayette Neighborhood: the "truisim about this neighborhood is that it was used for rental purposes, historically people didn't own their houses. I think that people have a different perspective as a tenant and a land owner." In over 50 per cent of the associations interviewed, it was taken as a truism that renters undermined the neighborhood.

Ultimately, that truism played out in a politics of NIMBYism. In Lake Carmel, another historically black subdivision in New Orleans

East, the association became agitated when VOB Development, a Georgia firm dedicated to affordable housing, began looking to purchase lots and put up affordable housing right next to Lake Carmel. The issue manifested itself as one of early notification. The association claimed it had a right to know that the project was being considered. The president of the association called it "almost scatter-site" housing – a reference to public housing sites in neighborhoods redeveloped in part to meet quotas as public housing was de-densified. The community used concepts of participation and community input to oppose the housing, arguing that they had a right to proper notification and that communities should have a right to respond when these affordable housing developments are being considered.

Seeking a broader coalition, the Lake Carmel Neighborhood Association reached out to the Eastern New Orleans Neighborhood Advisory Council (ENONAC) for support. ENONAC's vice-president explained that this was one of the primary roles her association played. If a single neighborhood association opposed the project it could look selfish, but when the entire coalition opposed the project, they were seen as an objective outside voice. "When they come to us they're mad about something. We have to take that 'mad' and make sense out of it." ENONAC took NIMBYism and made it politically palatable.

An entire infrastructure has been built up to ensure that NIMBY tendencies are taken seriously by governmental entities. ENONAC has relationships within code enforcement, zoning, and policing systems, and its vice-president considers the legitimizing of NIMBY attitudes by individual associations a primary part of its mission. ENONAC opposes the VOB Development project on the grounds that there has been no notice or mailing to notify residents, as Lake Caramel has done. Yet, just below the surface of this opposition lies the broader issue of who should live in the neighborhood. The Lake Carmel Neighborhood Association opposes the new development in part because it has a rent-to-own program. Originally, according to the association, the subdivision's charter did not allow for renting, though the rule was not aggressively enforced because of legal worries. The Lake Carmel president, however, argues that more renting "makes us work harder as an association." The vice-president of ENONAC similarly describes affordable housing, arguing that "development should not be intrusive." But what is it about this affordable housing project that makes it intrusive? The opposition to affordable housing based upon notification appears to be little more than an excuse to make a politically much more difficult argument – that the association does not want renters. In New Orleans East, ENONAC has risen as a political force in part to provide cover for this sentiment; the coalition provides the "objective" cover for associations to embrace NIMBYism tendencies.

On the surface, this opposition and strategy is ugly. Black, middle-class homeowners (like their white counterparts) use the right to the city to actively segregate their communities from a largely African-American renting population. The extent to which this is justified goes back to the arguments being made. Notification is largely a proxy for not wanting renters in the community. But there is an important distinction between opposition to renters in communities such as New Orleans East and opposition to largely white neighborhoods such as Coliseum Square or Fontainebleau. New Orleans East is already shouldering a large percentage of the affordable housing in the city. In Coliseum Square or Fontainebleau, the real argument is against creating a mixed-income neighborhood. But in New Orleans East, additional affordable housing has the potential to create pockets of concentrated poverty within that community, and research has shown such pockets to have detrimental impacts (Jargowsky 1997). Fighting to maintain income diversity is vastly different from fighting to maintain income segregation. The extent to which one sees activism in opposing renting in New Orleans East as legitimate likely depends upon whether one views NIMBYism as morally problematic or a necessary evil.

If neighborhood movements are to pursue justice, this tendency to advocate NIMBY strategies is a critical shortcoming of their interpretation of the right to the city. Purcell (2002) worries that by privileging geographic and neighborhood movements, the right to the city would result in even fiercer discrimination. Harvey (2008, xv) argues that "the right to the city is an empty signifier. Everything depends on who gets to fill it with meaning." What we see in New Orleans is that strategies based on geographic representation are a mixed bag when it comes to race issues. Protecting residents will sometimes protect people of color and/or low-income communities. But just as often, NIMBYism manifests itself against those same groups. If neighborhood associations are further empowered, if the right to the city manifests itself as a movement of geographically bounded associations in other cities and becomes a stronger force, that would bring significant risk for rental populations, low-income populations, and people of color. Neighborhood associations are not inherently on the side of racial justice. Just as other institutions (think city hall, school districts, development authorities) need to be pushed to consider and incorporate race into their analyses, neighborhood associations require the same push.

Within the Gentilly Terrace and Gardens Neighborhood Association, a minister who brought a branch of the Nola Church Plant to the community explicitly argued that it should be the mission of the association to consider racial justice. He argued that the focus on property values, blight, and neighborhood protection too often excludes people of color who live "across Mirabeau Avenue." His church then co-sponsored activities for the children living in that section of the neighborhood, did some fundraising, and convinced the association to expand its scope. Such transformations, also seen in the Irish Channel and in Broadmoor, are rare, but possible.

NIMBYism is deeply embedded in the psyche of the neighborhood association. Opposition to development is a powerful tool to combat Disneyfication, to protect the rights of residents, and to ensure the long-term viability of the neighborhood. But when such opposition is aimed at affordable housing and renters, the tool is a part of wider systemic and structural racism. At its worst, it is blatantly discriminatory and xenophobic. The same neighborhood protection ideal can be used to promote justice or to undermine it. The neighborhood protection ideal, the largest manifestation of the right to the city in New Orleans, is a competing priority. Sometimes it complements economic or racial justice, but just as often it conflicts with justice.

◆

6

How Far Will Activists Go for
Their Neighborhoods?
And What Does It Mean
for the Right to the City?

We came up with all kinds of clever things like that, it was just guerrilla warfare.

Kristen, president of the Northwest Carrollton
Neighborhood Association

It's how I got stuff done, I just called them, harassed the hell out of them.

Jeannette, former president of the Irish Channel
Neighborhood Association

What you're doing is wrong, and I'm going to embarrass you.

Jeannette, former president of the Irish Channel
Neighborhood Association

Theorists imply that the right to the city is an important concept because of its moral role in reasserting the rights of residents in their own community. The right to the city is seductive because of its promise to promote the vulnerable, to protect housing rights, to counterbalance tourism, Disneyfication, and development. But the very nature of the right to the city is movement-based. The right to the city has, thus far, been most useful as a slogan, not a governing principal, and rarely as a tangible right. The embrace of elements of this ethos by the New Orleans neighborhood movement shows how local quirks take center stage. Neighborhood efforts are one of *last resort* in which reluctant volunteers use neighborhood associations to leverage power across the municipality. Thus, the potential for neighborhood movements to remake urban politics is viewed through the lens of a particular political moment in post-Katrina New Orleans. Stepping back, it is fair to ask, is this the only possible manifestation of such movements? And, in particular, can these neighborhood associations be embraced systematically in a way that would alleviate many of the concerns (while keeping the benefits) found throughout New Orleans?

In many ways, that is a discussion about the informality and formality that mirrors discussions of the formality of social movements (Piven and Cloward 1979) and organizations using participatory democracy (Polletta 2002). In New Orleans, no one *gave* neighborhood associations formal municipal power. There were no rights for associations. Their impact took place almost entirely through informal mechanisms such as partnerships, protests, or (as we will see in this chapter) coercing existing processes, such as elections or public meetings, to enforce their neighborhood ethic. This maps directly onto wider trends in governance, economics, and philosophy that show informality as central to the ways in which governments work. Branches of these fields critique the idea of centralized management and control as problematic. But instead of arguing for a more localized scale of government, they argue for more participant influence in these systems through informal, not formal, mechanisms. Instead of imagining the role of the citizen as one of voting in a representative democracy, each of these fields reimagines the role of the citizen as one who informally inputs information into the wider system.

It is easy to see how that argument plays out in urban neighborhoods. In New Orleans, city council officers depend on neighborhood associations to inform them of blighted houses, potholes, damaged street lights, and any other number of issues. This is not local governance of the type Purcell (2006) warns against. Municipalities are not falling into the local trap (ibid.) of assuming that government is more democratic at local scales. Instead, this reimagining is about information. Surowiecki (2005) calls this the "wisdom of crowds," and it is already playing a critical role in our understanding of markets. Prediction markets, in which users can essentially buy "futures" in events happening (or not happening), often outpace expert predictions and have become a common tool in political discussions of likelihood. The wider discussion of governance is moving in the same direction.

Kooiman (1993) argues that the term governance has changed over time. Clarke (2002, 1, as quoted in Gaventa 2004) argues:

> Ever since Edmund Burke's famous speech to the electorate of Bristol in 1774 the British way of politics has been to leave decision making to the politicians and policy experts. The role of the public (or at least those who had the franchise) was to periodically pass judgement on their leaders at election time. This passivity has become an entrenched part of the British political culture.

But recently scholars argue that "[p]ublic policy is less a governmental dictum and more an ongoing negotiation among government and non-government actors (Katz and Mair, 1995; Castells, 1996; Blumler and Kavanagh, 1999; Ornstein and Mann, 2000; Bingham et al., 2005; Blyth and Katz, 2005)" (Crozier 2008, 3). Others, such as Stoker (1998), Forrest (2003), and Gunasekara (2008), argue that informality has *always* been key to governance and that scholars are just now understanding the ways in which informal systems influence formal ones. There is a growing consensus around the importance of such informality. For theorists, the challenge is to incorporate the role of such informality into theories. Sørensen and Torfing (2005) call this informal governance "network governance" and claim it has three characteristics: (1) governance involves multiple actors; (2) the actors are non-hierarchical; (3) the actors involved in policy decisions use negotiation as their primary tool to make policy. Network governance privileges informality – the actors need not have formal roles in a municipality or government, they need not have formal roles with one another, and they primarily interact through negotiations – a reflection of the same value found in informality by Piven and Cloward (1979) in social movements, and a reversal of the trend towards formalization in participatory democracy found by Polletta (2002). Deliberative democracy theorists argue that such problems can be solved via deliberations with the following characteristics: (1) reciprocity between actors, (2) accessibility to the deliberations, (3) a binding power behind deliberations, and (4) willingness of participants to change their minds (Gutmann and Thompson 2004). But these new-found theories must struggle with the dark side of informality. Dodge (2009, 225) argues that deliberative democracy research has "taken an empirical turn." Scholars note that leaving self-interest at the door seems impossible and may even be counterproductive (Deveaux 2003; Fraser 1990; Young 1990). In other words, with all this informality come power struggles.

Each of these theoretical developments (the wisdom of crowds, network governance, deliberative democracy) has a direct link to the right to the city. They each cite participatory budgeting as a manifestation of their theory. Participatory budgeting, popularized in Brazil, is a system of municipal budgeting that focuses on empowering civil society and even neighborhood associations as a check on government power and control (de Souza 2001). De Souza explicitly links the right to the city to participatory budgeting, arguing that it is a mechanism for social justice. Participatory budgeting is also an embrace of the wisdom of crowds – it is built upon the idea that aggregating local wisdom can produce efficient solutions. Similarly, it is an embrace of deliberation – linking citizens together and having them choose a binding budget for their community. And finally, although participatory budgeting is less explicitly a part of the network governance discussion, its broadening of the actors involved in governance, and the unclear relationships between those actors, all engaging in negotiations, is a manifestation of the theory. In short, the right to the city as it was embraced in part in New Orleans captures the core of each of these wider theories of informality.

But with informality come challenges. De Souza (2001) writes of the danger that informality could mean in embracing an "ideal" city without vulnerable populations, rather than one that upholds such communities and embraces social justice. That central issue of NIMBYism rears its head again and again in post-Katrina New Orleans. Informality also brings with it a question of legitimacy. What happens when an informal system breaks down? The question emerged in a new way in New Orleans after the storm – those involved in local politics were forced to ask, how far will activists go for their neighborhoods when informal mechanisms fail to heed their input?

Let us return to Northwest Carrollton where the local association was fighting development by a Walgreens and Roberts grocery store. We have already heard the nuts and bolts of that story, in which one neighborhood association recruited the grocery store because it was the last missing piece in its attempt to create the ideal neighborhood. For the adjacent Northwest Carrollton Neighborhood Association, the development appeared to disregard their community. It was not easily accessible by foot, it faced the street without a natural entrance for residents, and it even placed dumpsters alongside houses. The Northwest Carrollton Neighborhood Association found itself with few levers to pull to get its policy demands addressed. Here is the downside of an informal system. The development did not need the association's approval, and the support of the neighboring Fontainebleau Improvement Association provided political cover so that the development appeared to have community support. Northwest Carrollton was left out in the cold, engaging in negotiations but with little leverage. The result was an exercise in seeing just how far neighborhoods would go to create leverage in these informal negotiations.

Kristen, as president of the Northwest Carrollton Neighborhood Association, quickly became a thorn in the side of developers. As noted earlier, she called her tactics "guerrilla warfare." At one point during a disagreement with Walgreens over the layout of its development in her neighborhood, she went so far as to hang sheets at the construction site that read, "Walgreens Kills Neighborhoods." When such protests did little to affect the development, the association took another approach. It made Walgreens development a central issue in the local city council election. The association did the research first, which included a deep dive into the land-use qualifications on the corner lot. Armed with inconsistencies that potentially made the development illegal, the association convinced city council candidate Shelly Midura to open her campaign on the corner lot and make the Walgreens development issue central to her campaign.

In recruiting Council Member Midura (she would go on to win the election), the Northwest Carrollton Neighborhood Association provided a roadmap for how neighborhood associations deal with informality and negotiations. When included at the negotiation table, the association was happy to play nice. It worked closely with organizations such as Hike 4 Katreena, with which it shared values. But when it was excluded, the association became both creative and coercive. It engaged in a public protest campaign to discredit Walgreens. It researched arcane land-use requirements to arm itself in potential legal struggles. And it leveraged local outrage into a city council election. This last tool was particularly powerful in explaining what I call here "creative coercion." Cook (1972) coined the term in referring to creative strategies used for good, such as fighting racism in the South. Here, I redefine "creative coercion" not to refer to a moral direction, but to establish the manners in which less powerful entities (for example, neighborhood associations) challenge powerful authorities within the context of informal systems.

Creative coercion has three characteristics. The first is that this creativity comes about when an entity is actively excluded from a governing process. The second characteristic is that the excluded group must not have traditional, formal power (think resources, influence, or rights in a legal system). The third characteristic is that the lever pulled by such groups must be innovative; this is different from Castells's (2015) networks of outrage, which depend upon having greater numbers. Creative coercion is what happens when a small, powerless group becomes creative in an attempt to have a big impact.

In Northwest Carrollton, Kristen repurposed an election. She convinced a city council candidate desperate to be taken seriously by voters in the post-Katrina context to make *her neighborhood's issue* a key component of the election. Here, Kristen channels what Havel and Wilson (1985) call the "power of the powerless" or what Scott (1985) calls the "weapons of the weak." Lacking the ability to use force to influence an informal system, Kristen and her association influence the system by being creative and forcing those with more power to include the association in negotiations.

One key creative strategy is the repurposing of what is on the public agenda. Often participatory spaces are constructed. Lowndes and Sullivan (2008) call these spaces "invited spaces" in which government creates opportunities for participation on its terms. All across New Orleans, government created invited spaces. Testimony at city council meetings was limited to a few minutes, and residents were required to relate their comments to specific agenda items. Neighborhood associations were trained in how to contribute specific types of evidence to code enforcement hearings. The zoning board allowed for short, timed, public comment. Later, after his electoral victory in the mayor's race, Mitch Landrieu held meetings that allowed three-minute suggestions for the municipal budget. Each of these spaces was constructed so that participation filled a very specific niche. And yet, over and over again, I saw neighborhood activists flouting these narrow participatory spaces and repurposing them.

This was, at first glance, baffling. For example, at meeting after meeting, activists stood up during the space for public comment to complain about potholes in their community. It did not matter if it was a zoning board meeting, a historical preservation meeting, a meeting to which a police officer had come to speak, or anything else.

These frequent diversions frustrated public officials. Why bring up potholes at a meeting about zoning? Why bring up potholes to a police officer discussing a local spat of robberies? For those running these meetings, such digressions were frustrating, but they also pointed to a larger challenge. The potholes problem in post-Katrina New Orleans is real. New Orleans is sinking into the ground at a rate of 5 to 10 millimeters a year (0.2 to 0.4 inches), in part because the flood protection system interrupts the natural flow of sediment to the area (Horne 2008; Foster and Giegengack 2006). This wreaks havoc on the roads. After the storm, the standing water further damaged roadways. Faced with these challenges, residents looked to public officials to solve the problem. The participatory spaces were "invited" – that is, residents were expected to participate within narrow lines on narrow issues. They chose, however, to repurpose the participatory space. They chose to make it about potholes. Doing so maddened those running the meeting, but that was the point. If bureaucrats, police officers, and zoning boards were going to get their work done, they needed to address potholes issues, and none of the invited spaces included a conversation about potholes. So residents repurposed the spaces that were available.

This type of subtle repurposing happened all over the city. When the city council held a vote to demolish the Lafitte public housing project, the council chambers were filled with residents. Participation at New Orleans city council meetings is limited to a few minutes of public comment designed to help inform the vote, and on this occasion residents and activists took advantage of the meeting to stage a protest. They chanted. They resisted. When residents were kept out of city council chambers, they rocked the gates. Residents were pepper sprayed by the police. Inside, at least one resident was subdued with a taser gun. This became the news story. The protestors had taken an invited space, where residents were asked to contribute their thoughts on a vote that was likely already predetermined, and used it to garner media attention, which in turn built momentum for the cause (though that cause would ultimately fail).

This happens in less dramatic ways throughout all participatory mechanisms. Residents use the space for public comment at a zoning board meeting to talk potholes. Potential candidates for office use such space to build name recognition, and local activists use participatory space at city council meetings as a way of garnering media attention.

These types of repurposing are present throughout the neighborhood association action exemplified in this text. In Faubourg St John's, residents repurposed a legal requirement for parking to oppose a facility for people transitioning out of homelessness. The Northwest Carrollton Neighborhood Association did the same with a city council election, repurposing the election as a tool in a fight against what the association considered irresponsible development. Repurposing is often a critical tool of NIMBYism; associations with little actual leverage need to creatively repurpose an almost-unrelated aspect of the debate. In Sugar Hill, the neighborhood association opposed an environmental remediation program that placed non-violent first-time ex-convicts at the property. The neighborhood association looked for leverage to remove the remediation program and keep the ex-convicts out of their neighborhood, but they had little control over the property or what the university decided to do with it. At the same time, the university needed a zoning change for a second property, so that it could be used for offices rather than for faculty housing.

With little leverage over the environmental remediation program, the Sugar Hill Neighborhood Association decided to hold the zoning change hostage. The zoning board was friendly to the association and refused to allow the zoning change without neighborhood approval, which meant that the Sugar Hill Neighborhood Association had *de facto* power over whether the university could convert the property to offices. No one in the neighborhood cared about that second property; there was no preference for housing or for offices. But leaders did care about the environmental remediation facility. So the president and vice-president of the Sugar Hill Neighborhood Association repurposed the zoning issue and refused to budge until the remediation program moved back onto Dillard's campus.

Such repurposing is a direct result of the informality of these systems. Since neighborhood associations do not have formal power, they have to be creative to have an impact. This type of creativity is not limited to repurposing, although repurposing is the most common strategy found in the sample of neighborhood associations examined for this study. Associations often found levers where none were expected. Nowhere was that more true than in Historic Faubourg Lafayette in the conflict over a grocery store that would displace eight historical homes. The controversy over the development shared many details with the conflict over the Walgreens development in Northwest Carrollton more than a decade later. It pitted a preservation-friendly neighborhood association against a much-needed grocery development. Many of the factors in this debate should be familiar by this point. Part of the conflict was over design, particularly the suburban-style parking lots that came with the store. In this case, the NIMBY approach of the neighborhood association was supported by a local preservation-oriented nonprofit called Felicity Street Redevelopment Project Inc. This nonprofit added another wrinkle into the conflict, that of race.

Local City Council Representative Oliver Thomas (the latest rising star in a political machine in Central City run by former City Council Representative Jim Singleton) supported the project. It appeared that the developer had purchased all the property necessary to commence development. With little legal power and no financial resources, the Historic Faubourg Lafayette Association had no obvious means to affect the debate. At a meeting, Oliver Thomas criticized the neighborhood association's protest for being supported by white preservationists who did not live in the neighborhood, undercutting political support for the protesters. There were racial undertones to this whole debate, and although the president of the Historic Faubourg Lafayette Neighborhood Association, Jennifer, was African-American, most of her vocal supporters came from the Felicity Street Redevelopment Project Inc. and were both white and from the nearby Garden District.

Lacking public support, money, or legal influence, the neighborhood association set out to gain all three. Working on a local tip, its members discovered that one of the properties, one that the developer believed it had purchased, was still on the market. In relatively poor African-American neighborhoods in New Orleans, there is often confusion over the title to property. Properties stay in the family for generations and paperwork is rarely up to date. As a result, one of the homes that needed to be purchased by developers was available, even though the developers were unaware that they did not already own it. Sensing an opportunity, the preservationist Felicity Street Redevelopment Project Inc. and the Historic Faubourg Lafayette Association approached A & P, a grocery store that had been spurned in the development process. They elicited a six-figure donation from A & P.

According to Jennifer, at midnight she went to the family who owned the house and offered to buy it for $150,000 on behalf of A & P, even though the home was worth only about $20,000. They signed the paperwork that night and the transaction was complete. The next day, A & P donated the house to Felicity Street, giving it and the neighborhood association a stake in all future negotiations. The association claims that retribution was quick. Before the weekend was out, four fires had been set at the property. The fire department could not put out the last fire, and the house burned to the ground.

Jennifer was well aware of the danger inherent in her covert action. "[It] made us a target for a lot of ugliness," she said. "That's the risk when you go against the money people. That's what happens." Nonetheless, her efforts succeeded in bringing attention to the plight of the seven remaining historical homes, and the Preservation Resource Center ensured that they were moved to a new location. The grocery store was never built; the company thought better of it after doing additional market research. It was only years later that the empty lot became the site for apartments, developed by a faith-based nonprofit focused on affordable housing.

Here, creativity took a different form. The association was actively excluded from negotiations over development. Its values were ignored, and it was told that without ownership of the property, the association could do nothing to stop development. And so the association bought a property in a midnight sale. Such creativity is a direct response to *not* having a right to the city. Local residents did not have any say over what happened in their community, and to ensure a seat at the negotiation table they went to extreme measures. Late-night meetings and cash purchases were a consequence of an informal system and an example of how far neighborhood activists will go. But they are also a warning. The lot was not developed for more than a decade after the conflict. The neighborhood is still without a grocery store. In fact, it is unclear whether the partnership between the Historic Faubourg Lafayette Neighborhood Association and Felicity Street Redevelopment Project Inc. actually represented most of the neighborhood. If it did, the neighborhood was highly atypical, because, in general, preservation tended to be the concern of neighborhoods with more resources. Neighborhoods such as Faubourg Lafayette, with its lower-income African-American populations, tended to embrace development, in part because of historical disinvestment in such communities.

If bribery – the purchase of the house with a cash sale funded by a development competitor – was the creative approach embraced by Historic Faubourg Lafayette, we have already discussed an example of blackmail. In Algiers Point, Friends of the Ferry had little control over their local ferry hours. They broke their promise to devote toll funds to the ferry and coerced Crescent City Connection into extending ferry hours (see Chapter 1). In the Irish Channel, Jeannette could not convince a company to fire a delivery-man who was selling drugs. She used postcards, which everyone could read on the way to their destination, to trash the company's reputation and force a change. In Northwest Carrollton, Kristen hung signs reading "Walgreens Kills Neighborhoods" to draw Walgreens to the negotiating table. In Sugar Hill, Tammy and Maria opposed Dillard University's use of donated property for a remediation program for non-violent felons. They opposed an unrelated land-use change by the university to coerce changes in the remediation program. Each of these examples follows the same pattern. The neighborhood association has no direct control over what is happening. Worse, the association and local residents feel the program's effects despite not being involved in the process. The response to exclusion is to find an unrelated issue, a creative lever, and use it to coerce their way into a negotiation.

Perhaps the most extreme example of creative coercion took place in Northwest Carrollton. Kristen, the association president, became distraught when her neighbors did not share her concern about home demolitions after Hurricane Katrina. Kristen took creative and coercive measures to get their attention. Demolitions were becoming a hot-button issue as residents returned to the city, because blight and abandoned houses affected surrounding homes. If left unchecked, blighted homes could have a dramatic impact on those around them, not just decreasing property values but physically damaging the homes as well. Residents too often returned and repaired their homes only to have rainwater pour in from an adjoining blighted and abandoned structure. Residents fought rodent infestations that were a consequence of animals breeding in nearby blighted homes. In severe cases, blighted buildings collapsed, damaging adjoining houses. Where blighted homes remained standing, squatters and drug dealers often moved in. Some residents were vocal in wanting blighted homes demolished, but preservationists like Kristen were nervous about demolitions of historical homes and the potential abuses of power.

As a result of the vast number of blighted homes and their potential for damage to other properties, Mayor Ray Nagin declared emergency powers after Hurricane Katrina and suspended the normal approval process for demolitions. If a house was in imminent danger of collapse, it could be demolished on the mayor's order. Vicious rumors of mistaken demolitions circulated. People feared returning home from work to find their homes demolished.

Preservationists lamented demolitions, seeing historical housing stock disappear without oversight. Once a house was demolished, the city could always claim it had been in imminent danger of collapse. There was no way to tell from resulting rubble whether that was the case. In response, Jean, the Northwest Carrollton Neighborhood Association's vice-president, started a blog and posted pictures of New Orleans homes, so if a home was demolished, there was evidence of its condition beforehand.

Mayor Nagin's demolition contractors came under scrutiny, led by TV reporter Lee Zurik and fueled by Jean's blog reports, Squandered Heritage. The contractors were accused of charging the city for demolitions at non-existent addresses. That crisis would lead to an infamous showdown at city hall, where the mayor would point directly at Jean and say "[Y]ou are hurting the recovery of this city."

Kristen, Jean's friend and neighbor in Northwest Carrollton, was another avid preservationist who was also extremely frustrated with the demolitions and their impact on historical housing. But her neighbors did not share her concerns. According to Jean, that is when Kristen got one of her wildest ideas. Kristen knew her neighbors would not act until the problem reached their doorsteps. So, one night she went out into the neighborhood with a can of spray paint and painted the demolition sign on neighbors' houses. The next day the neighborhood was buzzing about unwanted demolitions.

Kristen's creative though likely illegal action garnered support for Jean's more public effort to reinstate a process for demolitions, rather than permit by executive order. Their ultimately successful effort is another example of neighborhood advocates using creative (though questionable) means to bring about a change in policy, despite possessing few resources and little formal power.

The pattern gives clear warning of dangers inherent in such informal systems. Neighborhood leaders are in their positions in part because of their fierce loyalty to their neighborhoods. Faced with an informal system that gives them few rights, such leaders will go to extreme measures to pursue their objectives. There is a tension here between imagining the right to the city as a right that resides in governmental hands to be granted when residents are invited into spaces of participation and understanding the right to the city as a movement asserted by neighborhood leaders. The principles of creative coercion provide a road map of how to assert such rights; neighborhood leaders repurpose invited spaces to gain a seat at the negotiation table; and they may go to extremes, resorting to bribery and blackmail, for example, while using traditional techniques such as protest.

Conflicts in the right to the city are often framed as being about power. Harvey (2008, 23) argues that the right to the city "depends on the exercise of collective power to reshape the process of urbanization." Balzarini and Shlay (2016, 504) argue that "the right to the city is about power" but defines power more narrowly in terms of "who should have a say in decisions about urban development." According to these definitions, communities typically lack power, and creative coercion is a symptom of that lack. If power is about "men going about moving other men" (Hunter 1969), then power within the right to the city might be categorized as *who goes about influencing a city*. That follows in the tradition of defining power in terms of decision-making (Lukes 1974), or when intersecting with a capitalistic economy, power comes in part from economic self-sufficiency (Emerson 1962). Studies of who governs in cities by Dahl (1961) and Hunter (1969) highlight similar power dynamics. By these standards, neighborhoods, associations, and activists have very little power. But more modern philosophical treatments of power view it as not simply one-directional. Political theorists such as Foucault (1978) explain that in every interaction, there is power pulling both directions. This dynamic is strikingly visible in New Orleans. Residents and activists find themselves entrenched in a bump-up system, without economic resources, legal strength, or any other traditional understanding of power. Policies affect these communities directly, and communities have very little formal recourse to change them. If power analysis stopped there, then neighborhoods would be glorified beggars, coming to negotiations when stripped of power and influence. But instead, neighborhood associations look for creative levers to combat exclusion. In urban neighborhoods, these levers ensure that power runs in both directions. There is power in economics, representation, and control. But there is also power in the persistent creativity of neighborhood leaders. That power comes from activists so passionate about their neighborhood that they are willing to spray-paint their neighbors' houses, or go night after night to public meetings, or spend money only at black businesses. The more directly a neighborhood is affected and the less empowered neighborhood activists feel, the more likely activists are to throw themselves into a messy, creative, and coercive attempt to be heard.

But the existence of neighborhood associations willing to exert their influence when actively excluded only reinforces the idea that neighborhood politics is a politics of last resort. These extremes are only necessary because neighborhood leaders feel excluded and do not have actual governmental levers to have influence in their communities. Given the hari-kari nature of such protest – the rapid burnout of neighborhood leaders and the creative extremes pushed just to have a simple say in neighborhood development – it is worth asking if there is a set of codified rights that might prevent a dependence upon this neighborhood-style politics.

New Orleans and other cities with active neighborhood associations have struggled to enshrine such rights into a city political system. It is one thing for the ethos of the right to the city – particularly a fierce parochialism that rejects outside control and influence in a city – to take root. It is another to find a way to empower neighborhood associations alongside existing municipal entities. In New Orleans, the Committee for a Better New Orleans drafted a Citizens Participation Project (CPP) that attempted to do just that. It included a funded set of boards made up of neighborhood leaders. It included an Early Notification System in which neighborhood associations had a legal right to receive information on development in their neighborhoods. The CPP also combated exclusion, excluding from the project any associations that charged dues. In other cities, such as Washington, DC, associations were legally registered with the city. And in Birmingham, Alabama, associations were funded for a brief time with $10,000 annually to put towards their own neighborhood projects.

These systems misunderstand neighborhood associations in two key ways. First, neighborhood associations are skeptical of such formality because it puts additional pressure on an already-strained volunteer infrastructure. The need to always have formal leadership, to attend even more meetings, and to keep up with the requirements of a formal system ultimately runs counter to the desire of neighborhood leaders to essentially have a local government that listens to them, so that *they do not have to engage in so much activism*. Enshrining these associations into government positions has the potential to starve them of the flexibility and informality that make neighborhood associations viable entities. Further, Early Notifications Systems and resources are still a long way from the mandate of the right to the city, which is that politics be fundamentally reoriented to promote the uses of urban spaces and communities for the residents who live there, often as part of an anti-capitalism movement. Such systems make it easier for associations to act in an informal system by guaranteeing them more information, but they leave fundamentally unchanged the informal ways in which such associations advocate. In other words, such reforms work around the margins to make the current neighborhood politics easier, but do little to change the underlying infrastructure of these systems.

Another approach might be to require that neighborhood associations give consent for neighborhood development, an enshrining of the informal system often used by zoning, land use, historical preservation, or code enforcement boards. On those boards, neighborhood associations are leaned upon to provide much-needed neighborhood context, and boards are hesitant to approve variations without the support of local residents. One way to enshrine the right to the city into everyday governance would be to set these as legal standards, not informal ones, and make support from neighborhoods an unavoidable piece of the formal decision-making process. But such a system would invite other problems. It would exacerbate the challenge of knowing if neighborhood associations are actually representing their communities, rather than hiding behind letterhead. And it would exacerbate the problems of NIMBYism, ensuring communities the right to exclude renters or vulnerable populations from their communities.

The informality/formality argument is, in many ways, a moot point. The ecosystem of neighborhood activists and neighborhood associations grew up specifically to deal with challenges to local governance and the disconnect between city politics and neighborhood interests; the system is path dependent; it would be extremely difficult to repurpose it into a more formal system (Peters et al. 2005).[1] The participation of neighborhood associations is similarly path dependent in that it is an organic response to the wider ecosystem of participation. Many neighborhood organizations have their roots in the localism movement of President Jimmy Carter's administration, which reinvested in neighborhood organizations (Fagotto and Fung 2006), but in New Orleans they are now directly responsive to the demand for more participation in government. That demand comes from public officials, who gain credibility from the support of such grassroots organizations. It comes from broader bureaucracies and parties, which see in participation a holy grail of politics with the potential to provide cheaper yet better services, but it also comes from residents who feel threatened by outsiders. Similarly, residents often feel disconnected from local bureaucracy and even local democracy, necessitating mediating institutions (Berger and

Neuhaus 1977; Boyte 1980). In New Orleans, neighborhood associations are one of the means by which residents address the need for mediation. If neighborhood associations were to become formalized entities with formal rights, another form of organization would likely emerge to defend local interests that extended beyond the formal rights granted to these hypothetical associations. In many ways, this has already happened; associations duplicate city council, which is a geographically representative legislative body. Neighborhood associations are what Chaskin and Garg (1997) refer to as parallel institutions – they are representative of communities that already have political representatives inside formal government.

Associations co-exist with city council specifically because of their informal nature. The technocratic nature of a city's legislative branch makes direct links to community difficult. Associations fill in around the edges and become a much-needed pulse to help public officials know what is happening within their own constituency. Given the parallel representative structure of associations and city council, there is already evidence of what endowing associations with increased rights over neighborhoods would look like. These associations were not built with the intent of governing, and if they were scaled up with resources and governing responsibilities at the municipal levels, they might very well fall into the same traps that catch representative legislative bodies such as city councils and grow to be technocratic and in need of mediating institutions.

Everything we know about neighborhood associations indicates that they are informal because they need informality to survive. Their leaders are already overwhelmed and experiencing burnout. Adding resources and responsibilities would compound those problems and contradict the reasons neighborhood associations exist – to advocate for and protect neighborhoods primarily as a watchdog. If these associations were to graduate to become more formal, similar organizations would fill the niche between them and the communities they represent. That was certainly the case for the founder of the Dreux Avenue Good Neighbors Society, who were concerned that their neighborhood association (Gentilly Terrace and Gardens Neighborhood Association) would not spend enough time and energy on their block, so they simply started a new organization to do that. Arnstein (1969) famously looks at participation as a ladder, arguing that tokenism is found at the bottom rungs. This is something associations and other activists certainly experience in New Orleans where participation and open meetings can be a legal requirement and little more than a box to check at many meetings. Delegated power, however, or even systems that give participatory communities citizen control can be found at higher rungs. Yet, the ladder does not account for the ways in which communities fight for such control. If the creative coercive actions of neighborhood associations show anything, it is that informal groups will continue to attempt power grabs when excluded from policy-making decisions. Participation always has the potential to move beyond tokenism or delegation because informal organizations can force the issue.

Informality is not only a means of balancing power, it is also a potential avenue for increasing traditional economic efficiency. Some scholars (see Box and Musso 2004) argue that informal participation can improve the efficiency of local policy by ensuring it fits the local context, mirroring Polletta's (2002, 2) finding that "[t]he sheer diversity of input into tactical choice that participatory democracy makes possible has enabled activists to outpace their opponents in generating novel tactics." Tiebout (1956) argues that policy differences across localities create a market that lets residents choose their ideal amount of service provision. In both of these systems, feedback through the local knowledge of residents is critical for sustaining the efficiency of local economies. Local knowledge is the key to unlocking logistical problems in neighborhoods that public works, police departments, or local politicians struggle to understand. Participation by neighborhood associations in policies such as community policing can form a bridge to such information (although, as Tiebout [1956] argues, the neighborhoods that do it well may then create contrasting neighborhood "products" that might lead to segregation). Given the difficulties that municipalities, police forces, or other bureaucracies have in collecting such information with a limited staff, neighborhood organizations play a critical role in providing local knowledge. Just as "prediction markets" – which allow traders to exchange shares that pay out if future events occur – are often an efficient means of incorporating rumor, innuendo, and grassroots knowledge into market prices, neighborhood knowledge has the potential to improve the efficiency of local service provision.

Neighborhood associations are essentially the infrastructure that evolved in New Orleans to play this role. In a multitude of small ways, whether through information about a spat of robberies, testimony for code enforcement hearings, advocacy to remove a pothole from local streets, or a database of blighted houses, neighborhood organizations provide critical information to a variety of municipal systems. One local activist told me an apocryphal story about neighborhood activists and their role in providing neighborhood information to the policy world. This particular story, while difficult to confirm, cuts to the heart of the contribution that neighbors can make to policy. Her story starts with the redevelopment of the C.J. Peete public housing project. During the design of the new housing development, developers insisted that in the new project all the houses face inward, with a central green space in the middle. This was explained to locals as a best practice. Facing houses inward decreases crime and mimics suburban neighborhoods.

There was only one problem. The residential association vigorously argued for the opposite, for houses facing out onto the street. To developers, without the context to understand what exactly the residents were asking for, this seemed a peculiar request. Public housing always faced in. Why were residents asking for something different? The answer demonstrates the subtle power of neighborhood activists and the local knowledge they provide. The housing project was along a parade route and its residents had grown up sitting on their porches watching New Orleans's famous parades march down the street. And the residents did not want that to change. The leaders of the residential association were basing their argument on context and history. This was not a political matter. It was a cultural matter. The best practice (inward-facing houses clustered around a central green space) did not make sense. It was a mistake that only the locals saw, understood, and agitated for, and in the end the housing project was built facing outward, towards the street.

In many ways, these apocryphal stories – I could do little to confirm this story beyond visiting the houses and seeing the porches facing the parade route – are the local way of cataloguing the impact of activism and of asserting the benefits of listening to local residents (in part, these apocryphal stories also provide a political justification designed to ensure those voices are listened to). These urban legends are the local echo to what we hear when a political pundit references a prediction market in a presidential election. They are the residue of the belief that small aggregations of local preferences and local knowledge can contribute to a thriving community and even outperform expert opinion. But these legends do not change the basic power dynamic that dictates that neighborhood associations or other organizations attempting to assert their influence must do so without the backing of a legal right and essentially while at the mercy of decision-making bodies. The examples in this chapter – of neighborhood associations acting through creative coercion to get a seat at the negotiating table – are extremes. Negotiations often end amicably, with collaboration and partnership as an outcome. Or, in the case of the bump-up system, negotiations can at least serve a watchdog purpose to ensure neighborhood concerns are met.

There are reasons to be optimistic about the potential of neighborhood knowledge. By advocating for more influence, neighborhood associations widen the scope of priorities within a host of issues, from development to policing to housing. Such a widening may make it possible to move beyond a zero-sum urban politics of right vs. left into a space where a negotiated efficiency can find compromise across varying value systems. This is a tribute to the potential of informal systems.

Rich (2008) argues that it is not enough to define efficiency as a ratio of costs and services, that we need to widen our scope of issues involved to truly understand the results of governing. Modern negotiating theory goes further, arguing that sharing information about values within negotiations is a critical strategy to increase efficiency (see Fisher et al. 1981). Fisher et al. show how disagreement about values can actually increase efficiency. If opposite sides of a negotiation agree on values, it becomes what is called a zero-sum game. That means that everything one side gains, the other side loses. But countless negotiations do not fit that framework. Plenty of times, when one side sits down to negotiate, it actually gains value: one side trades away things it values less than the other side does. The end result is that everyone can win, because everyone gains value.

That fundamental observation – that differences in priorities and understandings of value lead to better outcomes – directly parallels the potential of neighborhoods' knowledge. It means that these neighborhoods, along with their elected officials and bureaucrats, are not necessarily stuck in a zero-sum game with more powerful economic and political elites. One side's win does not result in losses for the other side. These differences in priorities are actually the foundation for efficient policy negotiations. If these negotiations with neighborhood associations can be reframed, they might hold the potential to find creative solutions that better represent neighborhood values. Hall (2004) understands this; it is the foundation of her argument for pluralistic evaluation in which efficiency is evaluated from the perspective of each actor influenced by a policy change.[2]

Any evaluation of neighborhood associations needs to do the same thing. Take, for example, the Northwest Carrollton Neighborhood Association's struggle with Robert's grocery store. By tweaking the design of the building, many of its most damaging aspects were limited. The neighborhood residents gained access to food, were able to walk to the store, and no longer had to face dumpsters or the loss of value to houses that such dumpsters caused. And Robert's, by moving to a more compact, urban-friendly design also picked up new customers from the neighborhood. Sharing information allowed for a design that addressed neighborhood concerns with relatively little cost to the business.

Understanding neighborhood associations requires getting their perspective on the outcome of policy negotiations. Anything less pluralistic fails to get at the key of the negotiation: the outcomes for everyone involved. It is a radical shift to equate neighborhood associations with policy negotiators (not as tools to produce better cost–benefit ratios), just as it is a radical shift to consider neighborhood activists as champions of a micro-local agenda rather than of a liberal or conservative one. The differing priorities of neighborhood associations are opportunities to gain value in a negotiation. The ability of neighborhood associations to create a vision is central to their importance.

Negotiation theory and local knowledge are cases for informality that parallel and bolster Piven and Cloward's (1979) argument that informality can improve the effectiveness of social movements or Polletta's case that a diversity of voices increases the use of novel tactics. But in many ways, these cases are not required for neighborhood associations to jockey for influence. In New Orleans, neighborhood associations do not exist, do not negotiate, and do not defend their neighborhoods because of a consensus that they contribute to the efficiency of a local economy. In fact, they exist despite suspicions from politicians and developers that they do the opposite. Neighborhood associations insert themselves into local negotiations because residents fear their local officials and local bureaucrats have become disconnected from neighborhood values. We can debate the merits of such informal systems, but the creative coercion of these neighborhood associations shows that local activists will insert themselves into these policy discussions regardless of perceptions. In some ways, that is a blessing. Associations can widen the scope of discussion to include new priorities, opening the doors for new policy compromises while raising serious questions about democratic, economic, and racial justice. In this light, the modest reform proposals, such as the Citizen Participation Project, make sense. The informal, advocacy-centric model of neighborhood associations is a piecemeal response to a system disconnected from the neighborhood ethic. Reforms largely work within this system, one that is path dependent. A dramatic shift, one elevating neighborhood associations, assigning them dramatically more rights, even funding them at much higher levels, would dramatically change the organizations. They would evolve from being lithe organizations fueled by volunteers and fierce neighborhood loyalty to being local governmental organizations or development-focused nonprofits. In that new ecosystem, it would be almost inevitable that new organizations would crop up to pressure institutions in the same way neighborhood associations do now.

For right to the city theorists like Harvey (2012), such an interpretation of the right to the city might be a huge disappointment. Harvey sees the right to the city as an extension of a Marxist class struggle that pits city residents against a wider capitalist system. For Purcell (2002), the right to the city is a potential reorganizing principle in the pursuit of justice for the residents of cities. But in New Orleans, neighborhood associations embrace only limited components of the right to the city; they make up a grassroots movement that ensures governmental accountability to neighborhood priorities. When a neighborhood association can pursue these priorities on its own, it does so. When a neighborhood association can pursue these priorities with consensus, it partners with government, nonprofits, and others. And when a neighborhood association is excluded from discussions of its own neighborhood, it uses creative coercion, repurposing participation opportunities to force existing power holders to listen. Thus, the manifestation of the right to the city in New Orleans is a referendum on the power of informality that stands in stark contrast to conceptions of the right to the city that emphasize formal rights (such as Mitchell 2003). It comes with the potential to pluralize our understanding of efficiency. It comes with local knowledge that can help ensure institutions and policies serve residents. But it also comes with the dark side of informality: the potential to be discriminatory, to shroud democracy or even use it to abuse vulnerable populations, and the potential use to reinforce existing power. This is the tradeoff inherent in the ways the New Orleans neighborhood movement actualizes the wisdom of crowds, deliberative democracy, and the right to the city.

♦

7

A Politics of Last Resort

The city is moving too slow. I do get disgusted every once in a while. It is a slow, slow process.

Kyrie, board member of the Pilotland
Neighborhood Association

Post-Katrina was the wildest ride in civil government anywhere.

Kristen, president of the Northwest
Carrollton Association

The post-Katrina New Orleans policy context was the site of many conflicts. It saw conflicts between economic elites and residents, between top-down planning, and bottom-up planning between bureaucracy and grassroots democracy. But it was also the site of a more subtle struggle, that between the ideals of the right to the city and the reality of local, geographically bounded activism. The promise of neighborhood associations in a city eager for local input to inform governance led to their rise in political importance, but it also put a magnifying glass on the flaws of a system dependent upon volunteers for governance. Yes, participation by neighborhood associations could inform policy and processes, providing local knowledge and bringing new perspectives to negotiations. But it also pitted neighborhoods against one another in the competition for scarce resources, stretched thin communities whose volunteers lacked the time to commit to activism, and empowered NIMBY sentiments. In other words, when New Orleans embraced its own neighborhood-centric version of the right to the city, it opened up a whole new list of problems. The New Orleans story, and likely the broader story of the right to the city, is not solely one of empowerment. It is one of navigating the tricky space in which participation comes with influence but few rights and the attraction of activists is a mixed blessing. For the residents who answer the call, this is a politics of last resort.

New Orleans's neighborhood associations serve as embedded cases within a singular New Orleanian policy context. With that come obvious limitations. The benefits of being able to move beyond one-off success stories or to be one of the associations with the most visibility are counterbalanced by the limitations of the comparison happening within a single location. But there are reasons to suspect that the political dynamics so visible in New Orleans are simmering in other US cities and beyond. A host of cities on the eastern seaboard are wrestling with Disneyfication. Cities such as Baltimore, MD, Philadelphia, PA, and Wilmington, DE, have invested in their waterfront properties, often choosing to focus on attracting tourism dollars to their communities. A snapshot of the Inner Harbor in Baltimore or of Brandywine Park in Wilmington shares similarities to the Riverwalk in New Orleans's French Quarter. David Harvey (2012) writes that new development on Barcelona's waterfront would be almost indistinguishable from those in other cities. These waterfront developments belie the wider apprehension that, as city centers attract young professionals and retirees, they run the risk of becoming play castles for the young and rich, not places of residence for those trying to work and raise a family in an urban environment. The pressures of tourism dollars and of gentrification into central cities put the dynamics of the New Orleans neighborhood movement front and center. So too does the global economy and consequent pressures put upon cities' finances. In New Jersey as in New Orleans, local educational systems are dependent upon the state for funding. In New Orleans, the state took the opportunity after the storm to take control of the school district. That same dynamic is at play in New Jersey, where the Camden and Newark Boards of Education are under state control with state-appointed superintendents. Philadelphia has seen a similar dynamic with an added twist. The state has so underfunded the Philadelphia School District that in addition to exerting state control, the city has been forced to privately fundraise for the district to ensure that schools have basic supplies. This dependency on outside dollars comes with outside influence – something with which many districts and charter schools struggle. In New Orleans, the influence of outside forces on a rebuilding city has been obvious and explicit. Naomi Klein (2007) calls it "disaster capitalism." But a disaster capitalism of a similar sort exists as a part of systemic pressures in the everyday city, both in the United States and across the world. The global pressures of competitiveness mean that cities face regional or international competition for companies, giving those companies influence in local policy. The same dynamic is at play between cities and states in the US context. Cities that are dependent upon the state for funding – something that increases in states with ugly segregation patterns – frequently find that local interests are subservient to state political realities.

All of this is to point out that while the demand for a neighborhood movement was explicit in New Orleans, it remains an implicit reality in many other cities. Other cities may not have a Green Dot Plan to rally around, but city politics often include influence from a wide variety of actors with interests that may not align with those of residents. Talk to individuals in neighborhood groups, residential associations, and other local organizations in these cities and you will hear a similar rhetoric to what was found after Hurricane Katrina in New Orleans. There is an emphasis on democracy, local rights, and resident perspectives, and the residents will be right to say that local organizations are doing critical work in their attempt to turn the balance of power back towards people who live in cities, not just towards those who visit or build corporate headquarters.

The existence of these underlying political dynamics and the possible emergence of a new urban populism based on the neighborhood protection ideal make it critical to learn the lessons of New Orleans that go beyond people power. Yes, it is important that we understand what Scott (1961) calls the "weapons of the weak" and what Havel and Wilson (1985) call the "power of the powerless." But it is also important to step back and think about the systemic effects of such power and the ways in which informal systems have the potential to reinforce existing power dynamics and thus limit their ability to serve as tools for justice.

Throughout this book, we have seen examples of this. Neighborhood activism has the potential to play a valuable role in the modern city. It is one of the few forces that will stand up to a development logic in which any development may be considered "good development" as long as it increases tax revenue and has a positive economic impact on the region. Such a counterbalance to development logic is critical to avoid abuses and poor use of space. Similarly, neighborhood activism is critical in protecting the neighborhood against Disneyfication, in which a city's economic system becomes so tailored towards tourism that the city fails to exist for the good of residents, creating instead a space that boasts only an elaborate theme park for those who can afford to visit rather than an actual city in which people live. By prioritizing neighborhood life, associations counterbalance the wider economic pressures of tourism. Neighborhood associations also provide critical voices when democracy breaks down and becomes technocratic or privileges development interests over residential interests. The associations can provide an avenue for neighborhoods such as Pilotland to ensure that forgotten neighborhoods are remembered by city services. This can be a vital equalizer. After Hurricane Katrina, neighborhood associations played each of these roles. Without associations and their neighborhood activists, residents of Algiers Point would have been left without a ferry, residents of Northwest Carrollton would have lacked access to a pharmacy and grocery store in their own neighborhoods, fraud and negligence in the demolition of houses would have continued throughout the city, historical homes would have been ignored in Central City, trees would not have been planted, the parks of the Irish Channel would have stayed empty, and Broadmoor might have become a Green Dot.

The activists, in almost all cases unpaid and with little to gain professionally, painstakingly volunteered hours and years of their lives at a time when they were heavily burdened with rebuilding their own homes and dealing with insurance companies. These neighborhood leaders truly deserve recognition. And yet what they will tell you is that this type of neighborhood politics – the type that leads a frustrated association president to call each day about a blighted home on her block, saying "it's how I got stuff done, I just called them, harassed the hell out of them" – is a politics of last resort. These leaders are worn out. Few have the energy to take on such a task, and those who do burn out quickly. Even fewer think neighborhood associations could take on more power and responsibility. Faced with the potential demand to provide social services, neighborhood leaders responded that they already have full-time jobs. The reason for their activism is akin to desperation. It is the type of activism that happens when a neighborhood is threatened, when democratic and bureaucratic systems have broken down, and when the only way to stem the rising tide is to thrust your own time and energy into the effort.

Look closely and see that there are also systemic issues to be concerned about, such as reliance on either neighborhood activism or wider informal systems in cities. These are critical tools for addressing specific injustices, but the same tools that can be used to stop a pharmacy from placing its dumpsters next to local houses can be used to oppose a grocery store setting up shop to a food desert. The same neighborhood association that organizes residents for neighborhood cleanups can organize a neighborhood against an affordable housing project. At times, these oppositions reveal the subtle challenges of neighborhood ideology. Residents feel the pressure of poorly managed social-support systems, and those who slip through a city's safety net too often end up in an unsuspecting neighbor's backyard. For a young mother living in Central City, dissatisfaction with the local shelter is real, as are the beer cans and needles left in her yard. Neighborhood leaders are correct to point out that the effect of their actions is often to restrict these types of institution, which may control unintended consequences in surrounding neighborhoods. And while this is true, it does not tell the whole story. Since it is equally clear that when a neighborhood has the power to prohibit, completely, affordable housing or services for the homeless and to outsource these challenges to neighborhoods with less influence or fewer activists, then the ideology of neighborhood protection often exercises that power. NIMBYism can be a force that limits the scope of development, Disneyfication, and even neoliberalism. But it can also be a force that limits affordable housing, public housing, and facilities for addicts. Structural (Friedman 1969) and systemic (Feagin 2014) racism have long been fueled by the desire to maintain neighborhood character.

In many ways, this is a story as old as democracy itself. Almost all modern democracies have sought to balance a direct democracy capable of ugly discrimination against the most vulnerable with a judicial system that protects the rights of populations that might be threatened by the majority. Paradoxically, the neighborhood movement can be used both to defend a city's most vulnerable residents and to bludgeon them. While theorists such as Harvey (2012) note that the right to the city is an empty vessel, and Purcell (2002) notes the risks that the right to the city might pose to people of color or other oft-exploited groups, little in the right to the city literature captures what these transgressions look like. The New Orleans case makes these transgressions tangible. It shows how the very logic that binds residents together against outside forces can also bind residents together against less fortunate residents.

This is not just a problem with neighborhood movements. It is a wider critique of urban governance. It is a critique of deliberative democracy, network governance, and the wisdom of crowds. It is a critique of the *weapons of the weak* (Scott 1985) and the *power of the powerless* (Havel and Wilson 1985). It is a critique of soft power and reveals a fundamental contradiction of activism. For neighborhood associations with little power, informal techniques to put pressure on government are some of the only avenues for change. Putting pressure on government agencies, appropriating elections – all of this power comes from the ability to "just show up." And the residents who take the time to do so should be commended. Such residents are making something out of nothing, which is worthy of praise and, sadly, often necessary. But these same avenues are often available to those who *do* have the resources and influence to take advantage of them. The same soft power that residents exert through creative coercion can be leveraged by developers seeking to change zoning regulations in order to raise property values.[1] The nature of power and money is that those who have it can exert even more influence on informal systems. Indeed, many of the examples throughout this text show neighborhood association leaders engaging in a type of informal tug-of-war between developers and residents. Worse still, empowering residents may mean empowering discrimination. Neighborhood associations are classically pro–law enforcement and anti-renter. The combination can be very unfriendly for residents of color, who are more likely to face implicit biases on issues such as when should neighbors call the police.

None of these critiques is unique to neighborhood movements, though the focus on residency, geography, and neighborhood exacerbates and empowers NIMBYism. Critiques about influence in an informal system stretch wide. And yet entrenching the right to the city within a formal structure has drawbacks as well. As with many conceptions of rights, the challenge is evident when rights overlap. If the right to the city is conceived of as a reorienting of urban politics around the resident, then what occurs when one resident's priority is the exclusion of others? Here, Marcuse (2009) may be on the right track. He explicitly argues that the right to the city needs to be defined in terms of the most vulnerable. Perhaps neighborhood movements should be as well. But this likely requires a big shift away from or a blind eye towards both the common use by activists of the right to the city as a rallying cry and of a neighborhood movement deeply grounded in property rights and home ownership. Focusing the right to the city around the vulnerable contradicts much of the strategic effort of neighborhood activists to remain informal so as to lessen the burden on volunteers. And coalitions built around NIMBYism may balk at such a reorientation.

Purcell (2002) conceptualizes such a reorientation, imagining the right to the city as a systemic politics of inhabitants that goes beyond activism or slogans. Here, we ask a similar question of the New Orleans neighborhood movement: what if the rights of such neighborhood associations were formally entrenched as a right within city governance? As discussed in Chapter 6, that type of formal legislative shift was explored in New Orleans. The Citizen Participation Project included an Early Notification System that mandated information about neighborhood development be sent to associations. Some judges in code enforcement cases or members of the zoning board already lean heavily on neighborhood association testimony. Formalizing these roles into a formal veto role is possible. At first glance, doing so might lay the groundwork for Harvey's (2008, 2012) anti-capitalist movement inspired by the right to the city. Formalized neighborhood association rights would provide a community anchor that is based on place, not capital. Likewise, it seems a powerful response to the wider New Orleans critique that locals have little power over changes to the city. In an era of city Disneyfication, in which development is specifically reoriented around the capital of rich residents and tourists, such an entrenched neighborhood right might provide an important counterbalance. But the ways neighborhood associations use the informal power they already have point to the ways that such an entrenched right might be abused. Devolving such powers directly to residents would empower those throughout the world living in slums, public housing, or other communities. It would almost certainly directly empower those who wish to exclude and segregate. The stratification of residents, business, and services would be systematically reinforced.

It is not hard to imagine such a world, because existing cities already feel such pressure directly. Residents would attempt to limit affordable housing and renting in their communities, concentrating poverty in other communities. Communities with wealth and expensive homes would be able to supplement funding for their schools, attract public institutions and private investment, be choosy about such a development, and avoid business models that undermine local businesses and jobs. Communities with concentrated poverty, facing extreme pressure from wider economic forces, would welcome almost any business, hopeful that the prospect of more jobs and less blight might start to turn around a struggling neighborhood. That neighborhood would be a patchwork of exploitative businesses, from same-day check-cashing facilities to industry that creates difficult living conditions. If such a system sounds familiar, it is because it already exists in many cities where the segregation of wealth into specific neighborhoods leaves others with little leverage and much need for investment. For these neighborhoods, neighborhood associations are one of the best means to leverage influence and resources for their communities, even while a wider system of such associations undermines their ability to compete for development and resources in the city. A system entrenching the power of neighborhood groups in urban neighborhoods is far from the only system that would lead to a segregative and discriminatory market, but it would likely reinforce these systems, becoming not a check on the power of capitalism in cities, but another manifestation of it.

Given that neighborhood associations are already at capacity, given their lack of volunteers, they likely could not withstand the type of formal incorporation into the city implied by a system that creates a formal neighborhood veto over development. Activists take these positions as a last resort, for a system that gives them formal veto power would likely require far more time and effort than already stretched-thin volunteers have to give. Perhaps the correct question is this: what system would need to exist in order for neighborhood leaders *not* to have to make this sacrifice? Is it possible to imagine a system in which existing institutions respond directly to neighborhood needs?

It likely is not. One of the biggest mistakes in studies of community is to assume that community has a single voice, a single set of ideals, and a single set of priorities (Ladson-Billings and Tate 1995). That, simply, is not the case. In fact, neighborhood associations are often testaments that communities are diverse and have diverse viewpoints. While the Bywater neighborhood was not included in the sample for this study, I often ran across lines of Bywater residents testifying at meetings about the city's Master Plan and Comprehensive Zoning Ordinance. The neighborhood had fractured into two rival factions, each with its own association. On one side, an association of largely younger residents pushed for additional nightlife and density, hoping to turn the Bywater into another hip New Orleans neighborhood. The second association was largely made up of older residents who had been in the neighborhood far longer. These residents wanted to maintain a quiet, almost suburban style of life where the neighborhood was a respite from the ongoing bustle of the nearby Faubourg Marigny (where Frenchmen Street was attracting more and more nightlife) and the French Quarter. In this scenario, which association is asserting its right to the city?

It is tempting to argue that associations should deal with such conflicts democratically, and indeed, many of them have the infrastructure for elections, parliamentary-style votes, and the like. But a democratic process dramatically tilts the direction of the association towards those with the time to volunteer, potentially prioritizing the retired over the working, those without children over those who have them, and those with flexible white-collar jobs over those with stricter work hours. Potential volunteers need to have not only the time, but also the inclination – a high bar given the intense dedication required of such participation. That high bar can also shift the direction of the association, giving its most radical or ambitious members a platform, since many residents lack the inclination to use such tools. Dramatic incidents like this are rare, but while it is difficult to prove, the wider history of associations fighting crime and blight is likely due in part to the selection bias of leaders. Those convinced that crime is a serious issue are more likely to volunteer, making the association as a whole trend towards a more alarmist approach to the issue than may be widely held. Each of these democratic limitations factor into the wider reputation of neighborhood associations as serving to help individual activists hide behind letterhead.

It is possible to institutionalize neighborhood associations, but difficult. Doing so without pay and professionalization further undermines the ability of such organizations to attract volunteers. They will likely buckle under the pressure. Professionalized associations raise a number of challenges – one is to meet the cost but a second is to distinguish their activities from those of the city council. Does formalizing local, geographic vehicles mean the creation of a new legislature? Assigning more power to localized councils of some sort quickly runs into the same problems that leads to activism in neighborhoods in the first place. When those institutions fail to uphold the specific neighborhood ideals of a faction of the neighborhood, entities will emerge to put informal pressure on the existing system.

Accounts that make these associations seem like white knights, saving neighborhoods by marshaling vast resources and winning local political battles, are flawed, just as accounts that paint these associations as solely existing to exclude and discriminate miss their wider efforts to build quality of life in their community. Instead, we have a neighborhood politics of last resort. Associations, embracing particular elements of the right to the city, are part of the city ecosystem. Most neighborhood associations are destined to fight losing battles, since the informal nature of their solutions requires access to resources and power that few neighborhoods possess. Their role is to protect their neighborhood. Some do that through a classic crime and blight strategy, others through more progressive means of reaching out to young people. Most advocate with their local government. And most are stuck in a no-win situation where, on one hand, associations are forced to use informal tools to craft influence, while, on the other, those tools – systematically – do not work to affirm the rights of either neighborhoods or their most vulnerable residents.

What we are left with is a more humble understanding of neighborhood activism. Gone is the promise of libertarians, that government could devolve and be run by neighborhood pseudo-governments. Gone is the promise of bureaucrats, the Big Society, and the faith-based movement – that community can create cheaper and better social services. And gone is the promise of the right to the city, a heroic slogan that represents the ways in which residential power could lift up those most in need of justice. In its place is a neighborhood politics of last resort. It is a politics that neighborhoods with access to resources and high quality of life are happy to avoid – it is not the richest neighborhoods in New Orleans that have the most influence. It is a politics that asks many days off work to be at city hall and many evenings away from family to attend community meetings. And it is a politics that those in power, from developers to public works officials, are often desperate to avoid. It is a politics that happens when something has broken down – when a street light is not replaced, a cherished local institution is not invested in, or a neighborhood becomes unsafe.

What the few neighborhood activists make of these difficult scenarios is truly remarkable. They use neighborhood associations as their vehicles to address what might otherwise be ignored. There is more power than one might expect in the bulldog-like persistence of a neighborhood activist who claims the mantle of neighborhood democracy. But just as with many other forms of power, that power can be misused. Just as with other forms of power, that power can be formed and shaped by those with the resources and inclination to do this. And just as with other forms of power, that power can be used to exclude and segregate. It is easy to imagine similar challenges applying to parallel neighborhood movements in other cities, but it is perhaps even more important to acknowledge the similar role played by home ownership, property values, and segregation in other movements. The challenges of neighborhood associations make visible the ways that these systemic issues are transposed onto activism and that activism itself can reify injustice.

In the informal world that swirls through urban neighborhood politics, there are few checks and balances. For post-Katrina New Orleans, the neighborhood movement was a necessary check on the politics of elitism that dominated the recovery. But it remains a watchdog, a check on the broader political system. To empower neighborhood associations beyond this, to embrace the right to the city as central to governance, is to encourage as many problems as they solve. Residents treat neighborhood associations as if they were behind a "break glass in case of emergency" sign. It is a painful, rarely needed, but exceptionally important safeguard. Those seeking justice in cities would do well to do the same. At times, the right to the city and the neighborhood associations that promote it are a valuable tool for fighting systematic challenges. But that same tool can be used to combat NIMBYism, quell (or encourage) neighborhood competition, and stymie critical development. It is a politics of last resort.

◆

A Methodology of Access

This harvest thus laboriously made, I shut myself up, as in a tight space, and examine with extreme care, in a general review, all these notions that I have acquired by myself. I compare them, I link them, and I then make it my rule to develop the ideas which have spontaneously come to me in the course of this long labor, without any consideration whatsoever for the consequences that some persons might draw from them ... as soon as I wanted to write from a preconceived perspective, to support a thesis, I lost absolutely all real talent, and I could do nothing worthwhile if I did not limit myself to trying to clearly render what was most personal and most real in my impression and opinions.

De Tocqueville, on intellectual autonomy, September 1, 1856

It has long been customary for qualitative researchers to include an appendix that lays out methodological challenges in broader detail while also serving as an explanation of the perspective (and more recently, the positionality) of the researcher. Amongst my favorite of these appendices are those by Fenno (1978) and Selznick (1949). These texts laid out what I have come to think of as a dance that furthers both access and rigor. On one hand, they describe the process of gathering and analyzing information, but they also describe the interpersonal interactions that lead to a deep, qualitative data set. That journey is personal and replete with the day-to-day challenges of qualitative work. I hope to do the same thing here, moving between the technical challenges and justifications, to the interpersonal. And, perhaps most critically, I will argue that getting the interpersonal aspects of qualitative research right not only is a moral imperative, but also deepens and strengthens the data gathered. Thus, design must consider the interpersonal.

That is exactly how I built the research plan for this project. The project was inspired by a separate research project funded by Dr John

DiIulio's Fox Leadership Program at the University of Pennsylvania. In many ways, I arrived late on the scene. I first started visiting New Orleans regularly close to three years after Hurricane Katrina. From the beginning, activists told me horror stories about "helicopter researchers" who flew in and flew out, never to be heard from again. They insisted to me, over and over again, that they were tired of people here trying to extract knowledge and that I needed to put time into the community if I wanted to be successful. The activists defined "successful" as doing work true to the community, beneficial to the community, and meaningful to the wider world. I leaned heavily on Fenno's (1978) text for guidance; he talked of stacking chairs after meetings and acknowledged that people chose to talk to him for their own reasons. At the same time, my project came with a host of tricky, methodological questions, including sampling, opaque information about neighborhoods, and real questions about the honesty of respondents within organizations.

Simply creating a sampling frame of neighborhood challenges proved extremely challenging. There was little criteria stipulating which organizations should be included, and many of the lists of neighborhood associations created by organizations (during the course of my research, I received lists from city hall, city council offices, the Preservation Resource Center of New Orleans, and City-Works) had old information and included many shuttered associations. On the other side, associations were starting (or were being revived) under new leadership after the storm. In each of these lists, as in the research on neighborhood associations, larger and better-run associations were more likely to be included, while smaller associations were excluded. This was not necessarily because of malice or neglect, it was just extremely difficult to keep up with an ever-changing landscape of informal associations, some of which represented just a few blocks.

A local nonprofit, City-Works, was attempting to create an annual census of neighborhood associations. At first, I had hoped to use this census both as a sampling frame and as a means to provide basic data on neighborhood associations, but upon closer inspection, it was clear to me that neither the criteria for inclusion nor the data collected matched the goal of academic publication. City-Works' original goal was to update the census every two years – something particularly crucial because neighborhood associations often have no fixed office or address and use the contact information of their president. With each new election, government officials or others seeking to contact associations would find themselves on a wild goose chase trying to track down the latest president. An updating and curated list could address that. But City-Works was also struggling with funding, and by 2010 it had largely shut down. I spoke to the nonprofit's board and came to an arrangement; I would perform the neighborhood association census, updating the survey questions to apply to this research, and produce a local report for those seeking an update of the neighborhood census (see City-Works 2010).

This report became the foundation for this research, allowing me to produce a local report useful for associations and other local actors and introducing me to associations through a local organization. It also provided a systematic foundation for sampling. I defined neighborhood associations as being geographically representative groups that included everyone in their neighborhood. (I excluded ownership groups like condo and homeowner associations, nonprofits like ACORN, and umbrella groups such as the Neighborhood Partnership Network and the Lower Ninth Ward Neighborhood Empowerment Network Association). I surveyed 146 active associations and over 33 others that were no longer active. Seventy-seven did not respond, making it impossible to know whether they had chosen not to or were no longer active. Along the way, I discovered many of the things locals already knew – that the informal nature of the associations made them unbelievably difficult to study or understand. In one case, two board members answered my survey separately and did not agree on almost anything about the association, from membership levels to budgets, to the formal name of the association! In another case, the president of an association informed me that the association no longer existed. When I published that in my report, I received a batch of phone calls from residents claiming they had been at city hall with the neighborhood association just the last week!

The experience reinforced the impression that organized and well-funded associations such as the Broadmoor Improvement Association are the exception, not the norm. For many associations, even something as simple as their existence was unclear. And this was partially by design. Many neighborhood associations intentionally became inactive for perhaps years at a time, but the informal network and name of the association still existed for times of crisis. In one extreme case, I reached a neighborhood association that the city had last heard from in 1998 – it still existed, but rarely met. Its members had not had much they wanted to do!

This informality extended to their understanding of their own membership. Defining membership was a constant challenge. The survey specifically asked for regular members, but many associations defined membership as those in a geographic area, while others defined it as their broader mailing list, and still others defined it as those who regularly attend meetings. These discrepancies mean that such data needs to be interpreted with care.

Nevertheless, the survey did provide an excellent frame for sampling associations. A key concern in that sampling was that lower-capacity associations might not respond to invitations to participate in the study or that the highest-capacity associations might develop research fatigue (more on this later). As a result, I drew a random-stratified sample to continue to collect research beyond the survey instrument. The goal was to use an embedded case model. Within New Orleans, there were 126 respondents to the survey, and from those 126 respondents, I selected 14 to attend meetings, interview leaders and partners, and analyze meeting minutes. I stratified the sample based on annual budget, a proxy for capacity. The population of neighborhood associations was divided into five stratifications. The five budget levels are:

1   $0–$100
2   $100–$1,000
3   $1,000–5,000
4   $5,000 and above
5   Did not answer the budget survey question

Associations were drawn from each stratum in rough proportion to the general population. The sample was proportionately drawn, with a final sample size of 15 in mind; the ad hoc sample size was large enough to include multiple members from each group but small enough to allow a single researcher to attend meetings and code documents. The only group that was over-sampled was the "above $5,000" stratum; these groups were the theoretically interesting pseudo-governmental neighborhood associations (City-Works 2008). Initially 14 associations agreed to participate in the study. The fifteenth association was drawn twice more into its stratum. The overall acceptance rate was 88 per cent (15 of 17). One of these groups later dropped out of the study, reducing the acceptance rate to 83 per cent.

The advantage to this randomized stratification sampling was that, at a micro-level, it avoided the limitations of studies in New Orleans that focused explicitly on success stories as case studies, and that, on a macro-level, it provided for a systematic, comparative study within the broader context of New Orleans. Individual activities and movements could be compared within a unified policy context.

A potential problem with the study stemmed from neighborhood leaders exaggerating their accomplishments and putting into question the general reliability of answers to interviews around sensitive neighborhood issues. Nonprofits have a tendency to tailor their answers to their audience (Stablein 1996). I suspected that neighborhood associations would have the same tendency. As a result, I wanted to ground these discussions in verifiable activities and also to place these activities in the wider context of the association's actions. So, from the smaller sample of associations, prior to interviewing I collected meeting minutes and attended meetings. As can be seen throughout this book, these forms of data collection provided important data triangulation; observation and historical documents on organizations can either confirm or deny narratives or explanations presented by leadership.

The study lasted for three years, starting in the summer of 2009 and continuing until the summer of 2012. I typically spent between five and eight months in New Orleans each year, mostly stretching the time over the spring/summer, with supplemental trips in December/January. During each trip to New Orleans I attended neighborhood association meetings, city council meetings, and a host of other meetings that associations attended (including zoning, planning board, code enforcement, and beyond), and met informally with local activists.

I also conducted forty-two interviews. The goal was to conduct three interviews with each of the fifteen associations sampled – two interviews would be with neighborhood leadership and the third with a partner of the neighborhood association. Of the forty-five potential interviews, forty-two local leaders agreed to take part in the study, creating a participatory rate of 93 per cent. These interviews loosely follow the Agency Profiling Method as described by Robert Walker et al. (1992). In that study, researchers came to local offices of an organization affected by a social fund and both conducted informal interviews with workers and observed their working practices. My interviews were informal and not recorded, typically lasting between forty-five and ninety minutes (see below for more on the decision not to record them).

For both interviews and participant observation, I used the Miles and Huberman (1994) system of fieldwork notation for investigation by ethnography and interview. This system involves taking field notes, writing up interviews, compiling interview summaries, writing periodic briefings, and writing theoretical propositions.

Field notes and interviews were informed by analysis of meeting minutes. David Mayhew (2002) uses history texts to ascertain the activities of Congress. Similarly, in this research, I draw from documents such as meeting minutes to analyze the types of activity that neighborhood associations undertake. The goal was to create a framework of activities that neighborhood associations are involved in that extends beyond big-ticket issues and gives a full accounting of their organizational activity. Ten associations submitted documents for study, one association promised but never submitted materials, and four associations did not have adequate record keeping for document analysis. From these documents, I compiled a centralized database of activities. Each action was then coded for a wide variety of theoretically interesting features, including but not limited to funding, decision-making, and representation – issues that connect the core questions regarding the right to the city surrounding economic, democratic, and racial justice with Knoke's (1988) categories of functions for associations: (1) service delivery to members, (2) education and public relations, and (3) political advocacy.

The participant observation, interviews, survey and document analysis were designed specifically to overlap and reinforce one another. The mixed-methods approach lent itself triangulation and also took the study out of a "whose side are we on?" (Becker 1966) space and into a "trust, but verify" space that fits a discussion of neighborhood associations. These associations are informal by nature and thus are particularly prone to being distorted by the lenses of individual perspectives. My strategy was to approach this issue by seeking multiple data points to confirm or deny individual perspectives (and also to be clear when analysis leans heavily on a particular perspective). The overarching goal was to use observation, document analysis, interviews, and survey data in a way to promote the type of rigorous, cross-cutting analysis rarely seen in the study of neighborhood-level organizations.

That process was informed by *standpoint theory*, which specifically seeks out and highlights voices, interpretations, and critiques from their perspective (Creedon and Cramer 2006; Collins 2002; Walker et al. 2009). Standpoint theory argues that when conducting research we must pay particular attention to community members and their interpretation of these events. In a similar vein, Becker (1966) argues in *Whose Side Are We On?* that too often community members are ignored, while the perspectives of privileged individuals and those in authority are assumed to be correct. As a white researcher conducting research in diverse neighborhoods, my own bias was the risk I took in conducting this work (see Duncan 2002), and I depended on a cast of local residents – particularly Jennifer Turner and others at the Community Book Center (New Orleans's oldest African-American–owned bookstore) – to help me interpret what I was seeing. Similarly, in "Research from the Underside," Holman (1987) argues that communities are too often severed from research objectives and processes, and as a result, research can be too technocratic and not address societal injustices like poverty. Each of these authors and theories points to a similar struggle – that local grassroots voices are too often absent from research. That is a starting point for this research. We can only grow to understand neighborhood associations if we start with their voices.

However, there has been sharp criticism that these perspectives can be taken too far. In particular, Alice Goffman has been criticized (Lubet 2015; Fischer 2014) for not triangulating such accounts and leaning on local perspectives without verifying their observations. Her approach to a state of the world in which authority is privileged is to privilege community viewpoints in the same way. In this work, I have taken a different approach, using multiple (largely qualitative) methods to triangulate data and attempt to capture multiple accounts of the activities and motivations of neighborhood associations. The research was built specifically to do so. Working with City-Works helped me break down boundaries with neighborhood associations. Collecting and analyzing meeting minutes allowed for an objective check on the narratives of neighborhood activists, but also provided a framework for questioning in interviews. Interviews could dive deeper by targeting specific issues or challenges faced in a neighborhood. Observation provided a similar check on reality. As expected, neighborhood association leaders often exaggerated their support within a neighborhood. These varying techniques built upon one another. Survey findings could be cross-checked with observations, interviews, and document analysis, and cross-referenced to new coverage. The goal was to provide a well-rounded, locally grounded understanding of New Orleans that could look at much of neighborhood association activity as a manifestation of elements of the right to the city.

It was quickly apparent that there was no existing quantitative data on the types of informal activity and campaign that neighborhood associations engage in while pursuing their interpretation of the right to the city. These activities were the core of the study – they drove the sampling strategy. They were also the best examples of these types of activity. So I set up the study to get to specific activities – which were then analyzed for patterns.

Collecting information on a variety of discrete neighborhood activities across a sample of associations was methodologically appropriate but interpersonally challenging. Haas (1977) argues that post-disaster contexts have four stages: the emergency period, the restoration period, the replacement period, and the betterment/ commemorative period. The emergency period relieves and protects citizens at risk. The restoration period restores public utilities, housing, and commercial structures, and sees the return of social and economic activity, including public transportation. The replacement period sees capital stock return to pre-disaster levels, and social and economic activity return to pre-disaster levels or higher. And, the betterment/commemorative period concerns itself with long-term planning and improvements.

My research project specifically targeted stages three and four largely because I was studying justice issues around policy, not the disaster response itself. But it also meant I was late to the game. Just as many residents were fed up with political outsiders coming to test their ideas in the city, so too were neighborhood leaders fed up with researchers doing the same.

Thus, a part of my methodological strategy was to be seen everywhere and repeatedly. I followed a rule that if I was invited to an event, I went, no matter what the event was. The rule took me to a midnight barbecue in protest of the Housing and Urban Development's demolition of housing (where it was rumored HUD director Shaun Donovan would show up, but he never did). I landed in pictures in the newspaper for trips to a PR event for the Lafitte Greenway and a protest for Charity Hospital. I set up chairs for some neighborhood association meetings, and took down chairs for others. All of this had dual purposes. The first was ethical: I showed up out of respect for the neighborhood associations I was studying. If they had generously taken time to help me with my research and believed I should attend a meeting, I did so. But this approach also improved the research. I acquired knowledge that helped me understand the context of local struggles. I built trust with neighborhood activists and received more-honest answers in my interviews.

The "being present" mantra became a core aspect of my research. My collaboration with City-Works was designed specifically to address local needs – a local city councilman's office was so pleased with my neighborhood census that they nominated me for fellowship for youth leadership. When New Orleans East neighborhoods were conspicuously absent from the census, I attended a meeting about how no hospitals had been reopened in that section of the city. Soon after, New Orleans East neighborhoods responded to my calls and were incorporated into my study. This type of local context was critically important for the work. As Holman (1987) writes, researchers do not engage only in unidirectional data extraction. They also engage socially, and interviewees often ask researchers questions. These types of interaction were particularly critical for me. As a young, white, male graduate student, I played into many of the gentrification and "takeover" narratives that my neighborhoods were worried about. For others, I was their ideal new resident, and they recruited me to come live in their neighborhood. For all, I needed to demonstrate a certain knowledge of the city, and for myself, a self-awareness that I was situated in the middle of the crises they were describing. It was a profoundly humbling experience, one that forced me to reconsider the reasons I was undertaking this work and the injustices I myself was perpetuating.

But in the end, this approach not only opened doors – generally neighborhood activists are eager to tell their stories once they get to know you – it also strengthened the research. The requirement that I learn the city's context in order to manage the interpersonal aspects of the research helped create a richer data set once the interviews were undertaken, and helped inform the analysis of the data I collected. Meeting minutes informed my investigation of associations. Participant observation helped ensure that participation rates would be high, and that I could understand divisions within communities even while they presented a unified front to the rest of the city. Given my efforts to understand neighborhood minutiae, it meant a lot when, close to a year after I had finished collecting data, a neighborhood

leader posted on Facebook that of the many researchers who came
to the city after the storm, I was the only one who listened.

The result of this focus on rigor, access, and ethics was a multi-
layered model. Within one policy context – post-Katrina New Orleans
from 2009 to 2012 – I surveyed 126 associations, selected 15 associations, interviewed 28 leaders and 14 partners within those associations, and collected document and interview data on hundreds
of actions that neighborhood associations took. But that was only
possible because of the standard that those within this study held
me to. Their insistence that I immerse myself in the New Orleans
context, that I work with local organizations, that I continue to visit
and live in the city over a multi-year stretch, all this opened doors
to a richer data set, but it also helped ensure that I would have the
analytical tools to understand what it was they told me. For that,
I am extremely thankful.

◆

Sample of Meetings Attended (Beginning 2010)

May 4, 2010 – West Barrington Association general meeting

May 5, 2010 – Garden District Association awards and elections

May 8, 2010 – DeSaix Neighborhood Association general meeting

May 8, 2010 – Bunny Friends Neighborhood Association general meeting

May 10, 2010 – Lagniappe Academies community meeting

May 10, 2010 – Faubourg St John Neighborhood Association general meeting

May 11, 2010 – East New Orleans Neighborhood Advisory Committee (ENONAC) general meeting

May 12, 2010 – Gentilly Terrace and Gardens Neighborhood Association general meeting

May 13, 2010 – Holy Cross Neighborhood Association general meeting

May 13, 2010 – Carollton Riverbend Neighborhood Association general meeting

May 15, 2010 – Gentilly Civic Improvement Association general meeting

May 17, 2010 – Coliseum Square Association general meeting

June 2, 2010 – Meeting with local researchers from RAND

June 5, 2010 – Lower Ninth Ward Neighborhood Empowerment Network Association (NENA) general meeting

June 12, 2010 – DeSaix Neighborhood Association general meeting

June 22, 2010 – City hall public meeting regarding the Master Plan

June 27, 2010 – Informal meeting with local author

August 3, 2010 – Night Out against Crime (multiple neighbourhoods)

September 7, 2010 – Fontainebleau Improvement Association
   meeting
September 8, 2010 – Gentilly Terrace and Gardens Neighborhood
   Association general meeting
September 8, 2010 – Lake Carmel Improvement District general
   meeting
September 10, 2010 – Informal meeting with president of
   Northwest Carrollton Neighborhood Association
September 13, 2010 – French Quarter Citizens Inc. board meeting
September 14, 2010 – Informal meeting with president of Algiers
   Riverview Neighborhood Association
September 14, 2010 – Informal meeting with president of Gentilly
   Sugar Hill Neighborhood Association
September 15, 2010 – Meeting with the Citizen Participation
   Project
September 15, 2010 – Informal lunch with local priest
September 16, 2010 – Irish Channel Neighborhood Association
   general meeting
September 17, 2010 – Informal meeting with president of Historic
   Faubourg Lafayette Association
September 18, 2010 – Pilotland Neighborhood Association general
   meeting
September 19, 2010 – Fontainebleau Improvement Association
   annual party
January 6, 2011 – Pilotland Neighborhood Association general
   meeting
January 10, 2011 – Informal meeting with French Quarter Citizens
   Inc.
January 10, 2011 – Informal meeting with Hollygrove-Dixon
   Neighborhood Association
January 11, 2011 – City Planning Commission meeting
January 12, 2011 – Informal meeting with Dreux Avenue Good
   Neighbors Society
January 12, 2011 – Gentilly Terrace and Gardens Neighborhood
   Association general meeting
January 14, 2011 – Informal meeting with the Broadmoor
   Improvement Association
June 6, 2011 – Algiers Point Association general meeting
June 7, 2011 – Fontainebleau Improvement Association general
   meeting

June 8, 2011 – Gentilly Terrace and Gardens Neighborhood Association general meeting

June 9, 2011 – Irish Channel Neighborhood Association general meeting

June 10, 2011 – Informal meeting with local academic

June 13, 2011 – French Quarter Citizens Inc. annual meeting and potlock

June 19, 2011 – Irish Channel Neighborhood Association, Lyons-Burke Booster Club catfish fry fundraiser

June 21, 2011 – Informal meeting with local teacher

June 21, 2011 – Lunch with former executive director of City-Works

June 22, 2011 – Lunch with staff member from The Lens

June 23, 2011 – Drinks with executive director of the Committee for a Better New Orleans

June 25, 2011 – Pilotland Neighborhood Association general meeting

July 1, 2011 – Gentilly Terrace and Gardens Community movie night

July 4, 2011 – Informal meeting with resident of Faubourg Marigny

July 5, 2011 – Meeting with Harvard intern at the Broadmoor Improvement Association

July 5, 2011 – Meeting with local fellow from the Robert A. Fox Leadership Program.

July 11, 2011 – Broadmoor Improvement Association Board of Commissioners meeting and Broadmoor Improvement District meeting

July 12, 2011 – Bywater Neighborhood Association meeting

July 13, 2011 – Lake Carmel Improvement District meeting

July 18, 2011 – Broadmoor Improvement Association general meeting

Notes

CHAPTER TWO

1 As there is no data available for the self-selected boundaries of neighborhood associations, the charts include data for the surrounding neighborhood for the year 2000 (pre-storm) and 2010 (post-storm). Race in New Orleans is largely white/African-American, so the numbers provided here give an estimate for neighborhood breakdown.

2 The Dreux Avenue Good Neighbors Society is an association launched within the territory of Gentilly Terrace. Thus, the neighborhood data (which covers the entire neighborhood as defined by the city, not just as defined by the association) is the same.

CHAPTER THREE

1 This is a shift from Edsall and Blumgart's definitions of new urban populism, which sees it as a progressive shift to the left. I argue that new urban populism is indicative of a neighborhood ideal that often is a non-ideological component of a progressive coalition.

2 This practice was ended when hiring off-duty police officers was made illegal in response to a scandal in which the New Orleans Police Department was assigning on-duty officers to these neighborhoods – essentially double-dipping.

CHAPTER FOUR

1 This is exactly the type of NIMBY activity discussed in Chapter 5.

2 This struggle over the association agenda reflects the findings in Chapter 3 about crime and blight associations, as well as the role of faith-based institutions.

CHAPTER FIVE

1 This is not universally true. Some primarily white neighborhoods, like Lakeview, were very susceptible to flooding.

CHAPTER SIX

1 Peters et al. (2005) write of path dependency in policy. Classically, path dependency has referred to policies that, once on a particular track, are very difficult to change. For example, in the United States, Social Security provides pension-like payments to current retirees using the tax contributions of current workers. While it is hypothetically possible to imagine a system that saves contributions of current workers, then gives that money back to those workers when they retire, it is not feasible to get to that system from the current policy because it would require finding the money to pay for all those current retirees whose contributions have already been spent on payouts to past retirees, all while saving current tax contributions. In other words, the original structure of the policy means that it is almost impossible to jump streams and fund the system in an entirely different way. The policy is "path dependent."

2 Pluralistic evaluation was specifically developed in the health-care sector and seeks to evaluate health-care outcomes in terms of all the actors involved. It may be the case that patients (pluralistic evaluation) have a fundamentally different view of what is more important than health-care professionals or policy-makers. Thus, if providers only use one perception of priorities, they could think a program was a success even when its patients consider it a failure. Pluralistic evaluation fixes that perception by evaluating the program from the perspective of everyone involved.

CHAPTER SEVEN

1 This is a particular problem in the French Quarter, where speculators once bought properties on North Rampart Street knowing that if proposed zoning changes allowed Rampart to be zoned for entertainment such as that on Bourbon Street, the properties would immediately jump in value.

References

Abzug, Rikki. 2008. "Community elites and power structure." In *Handbook of Community Movements and Local Organizations*, 89–101. Boston, MA: Springer.

Adams, Vicanne. 2013. *Markets of Sorrow, Labors of Faith: New Orleans in the Wake of Katrina*. Durham, NC: Duke University Press.

Adler, David. 2015. "Do we have a right to the city?" *Jacobin*. Accessed October 1, 2016: https://www.jacobinmag.com/2015/10/mexico-city-df-right-to-the-city-harvey-gentrification-real-estate-corruption

Alexander, Michelle. 2012. *The New Jim Crow: Mass Incarceration in the Age of Colorblindness*. The New Press.

Alinsky, Saul. 1971. *Rules for Radicals: A Practical Primer for Realistic Radicals*. New York, NY: Vintage.

Angotti, Tom. 2009. "The right to the city versus bridging the urban divide." *The Urban Reinventors* 3. Available at: http://www.rbanreinventors.net/3/angotti/angotti-urbanreinventors.pdf

Anheier, Helmut K., and Lester Salamon. 2006. "The nonprofit sector in comparative perspective." In *The Nonprofit Sector: A Research Handbook*, edited by Walter Powell and Richard Steinberg, 89–113. New Haven, CT: Yale University Press.

Arena, John. 2012. *Driven from New Orleans: How Nonprofits Betray Public Housing and Promote Privatization*. Minneapolis, MN: University of Minnesota Press.

Arnold, Joseph. 1979. "The neighborhood and City Hall." *Journal of Urban History* 6, no. 1: 3–30.

Arnstein, Sherry. 1969. "A ladder of citizen participation." *Journal of the American Planning Association* 35, no. 4: 216–24.

Ascher, Lois. 2009. "Enacting democracy – public space: Theater of discourse." *The Urban Reinventors* 3. Available at: http://www.urbanreinventors.net/paper.php?issue=3&author=ascher

Attoh, Kafui. 2011. "What kind of right is the right to the city?" *Progress in Human Geography* 35, no. 5: 669–85.

Austin, Mark. 1991. "Community context and complexity of organizational structure in neighborhood associations." *Administration & Society* 22, no. 4: 516–31.

Balzarini, John, and Anne Shlay. 2016. "Gentrification and the right to the city: Community conflict and casinos." *Journal of Urban Affairs* 38, no. 4: 503–17.

Barbaro, Michael. 2013. "Bloomberg focuses on the rest (as in rest of the world)." *New York Times*, December 14.

Barry, Jon. 1998. *Rising Tide: The Great Mississippi Flood of 1927 and How It Changed America*. New York, NY: Simon and Schuster.

Becker, Howard. 1966. "Whose side are we on?" *Social Problems* 14: 239.

Berger, Peter, and Richard John Neuhaus. 1977. "To empower people: The role of mediating structures in public policy." American Enterprise Institute for Public Policy Research. Washington, DC, 1.

Berkshire, Jennifer. 2014. "Lab rats." *Have You Heard Blog*. Available at http://edushyster.com/?p=5006

Bingham, Lisa Blomgren, Tina Nabatchi, and Rosemary O'Leary. 2005. "The new governance: Practices and processes for stakeholder and citizen participation in the work of government." *Public Administration Review* 65, no. 5: 547–58.

Birkland, Thomas. 2006. *Lessons of Disaster: Policy Change after Catastrophic Events*. Washington, DC: Georgetown University Press.

Blau, Peter Michael, and W. Richard Scott. 1962. *Formal Organizations: A Comparative Approach*. Stanford, CA: Stanford Business Books.

Blumgart, Jake. 2013. "The year of the urban populist." In *Next City*. Accessed February 3, 2018: https://nextcity.org/daily/entry/the-year-of-the-urban-populist

Blumler, Jay G., and Dennis Kavanagh. 1999. "The third age of political communication: Influences and features." *Political Communication* 16, no. 3: 209–30.

Blyth, Mark, and Richard Katz. 2005. "From catch-all politics to cartelisation: The political economy of the cartel party." *West European Politics* 28, no. 1: 33–60.

Bonilla-Silva, Eduardo. 2010. *Racism without Racists: Color-Blind Racism and the Persistence of Racial Inequality in the United States*. New York,

NY: Rowman & Littlefield.Bourne, Joel. 2004. "Gone with the water." *National Geographic*. Accessed February 3, 2018: http://ngm.national-geographic.com/ngm/0410/feature5/text2.html

Box, Richard C., and Juliet Ann Musso. 2004. "Experiments with local federalism." *American Review of Public Administration* 34, no. 3: 259–76.

Boyte, Harry. 1980. *The Backyard Revolution: Understanding the New Citizen Movement*. Philadelphia, PA: Temple University Press.

Brandt, Richard B. 1962. *Social Justice*. Englewood Cliffs, NJ: Prentice-Hall.

Broadmoor Project. 2007. "Lessons from Katrina: How a community can spearhead successful disaster recovery." John F. Kennedy School of Government, Harvard University, Cambridge, MA. Accessed at http://belfercenter.ksg.harvard.edu/files/uploads/DisasterRecoveryGuide_Phase_1.pdf

Brown, Kerry, and Robin Keast. 2003. "Citizen-government engagement: Community connection through networked arrangements." *Asian Journal of Public Administration* 25, no. 1: 107–32.

Buckley, Eileen. 2014. "City school leader holds listening tour." *WBFO 88.7 NPR Buffalo*. Accessed February 3, 2018, at http://news.wbfo.org/post/city-school-leader-holds-listening-tour

Building Big Society. 2010. "Building big society." *United Kingdom Cabinet Office*. Accessed February 3, 2018: http://www.cabinetoffice.gov.uk/sites/default/files/resources/building-big-society_0.pdf

Buras, Kristen. 2014. *Charter Schools, Race, and Urban Space: Where the Market Meets Grassroots Resistance*. New York, NY: Routledge.

Buroni, T. 1998. "A case for the right to habitat." A paper presented at a conference on seminar on urban poverty, Rio de Janeiro. Unpublished manuscript as in Purcell 2002.

Busà, Alessandro. 2009. "The right to the city: The entitled and the excluded." *Urban Reinventors* 3, no. 9: 1–13.

Castells, Manuel. 1996. *Rise of the Network Society: The Information Age: Economy, Society and Culture* (Vol. 1). Oxford, UK: Blackwell Publishers.

– 2015. *Networks of Outrage and Hope: Social Movements in the Internet Age*. Edison, NJ: John Wiley & Sons.

Chamlee-Wright, Emily. 2008. "Signaling effects of commercial and civil society in post-Katrina reconstruction." *International Journal of Social Economics* 35, no. 8: 615–26.

Chamlee-Wright, Emily, and Virgil Storr. 2009. "The role of social entrepreneurship in post-disaster recovery." *International Journal of Innovation and Regional Development* 2, no. 1: 149–64.

Chaskin, Robert J., and Sunil Garg. 1997. "The issue of governance in neighborhood-based initiatives." *Urban Affairs Review* 32, no. 5: 631–61.

Chetkovich, Carol A., and Frances Kunreuther. 2006. *From the Ground Up: Grassroots Organizations Making Social Change*. Ithaca, NY: Cornell University Press.

Cigler, Beverly. 2001. "Multiorganizational, multisector, and multicommunity organizations: Setting the research agenda." In *Getting Results through Collaboration: Networks and Network Structures for Public Policy and Management*, edited by Myrna Mandell, 71–85. Westport, CT: Quorum Books.

Cities for Human Rights. 1998. Conference in Barcelona, October. As in Purcell 2002.

City & Shelter. N.d. "The European charter for women in the city." Unpublished manuscript as in Purcell 2002.

City-Works. 2008. "Mapping of New Orleans: Neighborhood organizations and their reinvigoration in the face of government inaction." *City Works*. Blue Moon Fund.

– 2010. "The Neighborhood Mapping Project." *City Works*.

Clarke, Richard, 2002. "Public participation in the UK." In a paper presented for Conference on Spaces and Places of Participation, Institute of Development Studies, October. As in Gaventa 2004.

Cnaan, Ram A. 2006. *The Other Philadelphia Story: How Local Congregations Support Quality of Life in Urban America*. Philadelphia, PA: University of Pennsylvania Press.

Collins, Patricia Hill. 2002. *Black Feminist Thought: Knowledge, Consciousness, and the Politics of Empowerment*. New York, NY: Routledge.

Cook, Samuel. 1972. "Coercion and social change." In *Coercion*, NOMOS XIV: 107–43. Chicago: Aldine-Atherton.

Creedon, Pamela J., and Judith Cramer. 2006. *Women in Mass Communication*. Washington, DC: Sage Publications.

Crozier, Michael. 2008. "Listening, learning, steering: New governance, communication and interactive policy formation." *Policy & Politics* 36, no. 1: 3–19.

Cunningham, Andy. 2015. "Actor, New Orleanian Wendell Pierce takes on neighborhood association." *WDSU News*. Accessed February 3, 2018: http://www.wdsu.com/news/local-news/new-orleans/actor-new-orleanian-wendell-pierce-takes-on-neighborhood-association/34206804?

Dahl, Robert A. 1961. *Who Governs? Democracy and Power in an American City*. New Haven, CT: Yale University Press.

Daka-Mulwanda, Vai, Kathy R. Thornburg, Laura Filbert, and Tanna Klein. 1995. "Collaboration of services for children and families: A synthesis of recent research and recommendations." *Family Relations* 44, no. 2: 219–23.

Daniel, Celso. 2001. "Participatory urban governance: The experience of Santo Andre." *Un Chronicle* 38, no. 1: 28–9.

Daniels, R. Steven. 2007. "Revitalizing emergency management after Katrina." *Public Manager* 36, no. 3: 16.

Davis, Mike. 1990. *City of Quartz: Excavating the Future in Los Angeles.* London, UK: Vintage.

Davis, Phil. 2014, "Gov. Christie, Camden superintendent tout new after school dinner program." *NJ.com.* Accessed February 3, 2018: http://www.nj.com/camden/index.ssf/2014/01/gov_christie_camden_superintendent_tout_new_after_school_dinner_program.html

Delmont, Matthew. 2016. *Why Busing Failed: Race, Media, and the National Resistance to School Desegregation.* Oakland, CA: University of California Press.

DeSalvo, Karen. 2010. "Community health clinics: Bringing quality care closer to New Orleanians." In *The New Orleans Index at Five*, edited by Amy Liu and Allison Plyer. Washington, DC: Brookings Press.

de Souza, Marecelos Lopes. 2001. "The Brazilian way of conquering the 'right to the city' successes and obstacles in the long stride towards an 'Urban reform.'" *disP – the Planning Review* 37, no. 147: 25–31.

Deveaux, Monique. 2003. "A deliberative approach to conflicts of culture." *Political Theory* 31, no. 6: 780–807.

DiIulio, John. 2007. *Godly Republic: A Centrist Civic Blueprint for America's Faith-Based Future,* Berkeley, CA: University of California Press.

Dodge, Jennifer. 2009. "Environmental justice and deliberative democracy: How social change organizations respond to power in the deliberative system." *Policy and Society* 28, no. 3: 225–39.

Douglas, Mary. 1991. *Purity and Danger: An Analysis of Concepts of Pollution and Taboo.* Routledge.

Duncan, Garrett Albert. 2002. "Critical race theory and method: Rendering race in urban ethnographic research." *Qualitative Inquiry* 8, no. 1: 85–104.

Dyson, Michael Eric, and Paul Elliott. 2010. *Come Hell or High Water: Hurricane Katrina and the Color of Disaster.* ReadHowYouWant.com

Edsall, Thomas. 2013. "Bill de Blasio and the new urban populism." *New York Times.* October 22, 2013.

Eldridge, John Eric Thomas, and Alastair Crombie. 1974. *A Sociology of Organisations.* New York, NY: Routledge.

Emerson, Richard. 1962. "Power-dependence relations." *American Sociological Review* 27, no. 1: 31–41.

Fagotto, Elena, and Archon Fung. 2006. "Empowered participation in urban governance: The Minneapolis neighborhood revitalization program." *International Journal of Urban and Regional Research* 30, no. 3: 638–55.

Fainstein, Norman I., and Susan Fainstein. 1974. *Urban Political Movements: The Search for Power by Minority Groups in American Cities*. Upper Sadler River, NJ: Prentice Hall.

Feagin, Joe. 2014. *Racist America: Roots, Current Realities, and Future Reparations*. New York, NY: Routledge.

Fenno, Richard. 1978. *Home Style: House Members in Their Districts*. Boston, MA: Little, Brown.

Fine, Michael. 2001. "The New South Wales demonstration projects." In *Getting Results through Collaboration: Networks and Network Structures for Public Policy and Management*, edited by Myrna Mandell, 207. Westport, CT: ABC-Clio.

Fischer, Claude. 2014. "Slumming it." *Boston Review* 39, no. 6: 8.

Fischer, Roger, William Ury, and Bruce Patton. 1981. *Getting to Yes: Negotiating Agreement without Giving*. New York, NY: Penguin Press.

Ford, Kristina. 2010. *The Trouble with City Planning: What New Orleans Can Teach Us*. New Haven, CT: Yale University Press.

Forrest, Joshua B. 2003. "Networks in the policy process: An international perspective." *International Journal of Public Administration* 26, no. 6: 591–608.

Foster, Kenneth, and Robert Giegengack. 2006. "Planning for a city on the brink." In *On Risk and Disaster: Lessons from Hurricane Katrina*, edited by Robert Daniels, Donald Kettl, and Howard Kunreuther, 41. Philadelphia, PA: University of Pennsylvania Press.

Foucault, Michael. 1978. *The History of Sexuality*. New York, NY: Pantheon Books.

Frankena, William K. 1962. "The concept of social justice." *Social Justice* 1: 17.

Fraser, Nancy. 1990. "Rethinking the public sphere: A contribution to the critique of actually existing democracy." *Social Text*, nos 25–6: 56–80.

Freeman, Jo. 1972. "The tyranny of structurelessness." *Berkeley Journal of Sociology* 17: 151–64.

Friedman, Samuel. 1969. "How is racism maintained?" *Et Al* 2: 18–21.

Fussell, Elizabeth, Narayan Sastry, and Mark VanLandingham. 2010. "Race, socioeconomic status, and return migration to New Orleans after Hurricane Katrina." *Population and Environment* 31, nos 1–3: 20–42.

Gaventa, John. 2004. "Representation, community leadership and participation: Citizen involvement in neighbourhood renewal and local governance." Paper prepared for Neighbourhood Renewal Unit Office of Deputy Prime Minister, London, UK: July.

Gibson, Katherine, and Jenny Cameron. 2001. "Transforming communities: Towards a research agenda." *Urban Policy and Research* 19, no. 1: 7–24.

Gladwell, Malcolm. 2000. *The Tipping Point: How Little Things Can Make a Big Difference*. New York, NY: Little, Brown and Company.

Grant Building Tenants Association. 2001. "Grant building saved (for the moment)." Grant Building Tenants Association, San Francisco. As in Purcell 2002.

Gratz, Roberta Brandes. 2015. *We're Still Here Ya Bastards: How the People of New Orleans Rebuilt Their City*. New York, NY: Nation Books.

Greenwald, Anthony, and Linda Hamilton Krieger. 2006. "Implicit bias: Scientific foundations." *California Law Review* 94, no. 4: 945–67.

Gunasekara, Chrys. 2008. *Network Governance amidst Local Economic Crisis*. London, UK: Taylor Francis Ltd.

Gutmann, A., and D. Thompson. 2002. "Deliberative democracy beyond process." *Journal of Political Philosophy* 10, no. 2: 153–74.

– 2004. *Why Deliberative Democracy*. Princeton, NJ: Princeton University Press.

Haas, J. Eugene, Robert Kates, and Martyn Bowden. 1977. *Reconstruction Following Disaster*. Boston, MA: MIT Press.

Hajer, Martin. 2003. *Deliberative Policy Analysis: Understanding Governance in the Network Society*. Cambridge, UK: Cambridge University Press.

Hall, Julie. 2004. "Pluralistic evaluation: A situational approach to service evaluation." *Journal of Nursing Management* 12, no. 1: 22–7.

Hancock, Alexander. 2011. "Bacchanal shut down for operating without proper permits – DHH Chronicles." Accessed February 3, 2018: http://nola.eater.com/archives/2011/08/31/bacchanal-shut-down-for-operating-without-proper-permits.php

Hartman, Chester, and Gregory Squires. 2006. *There Is No Such Thing as a Natural Disaster: Race, Class, and Hurricane Katrina*. Abingdon, UK: Taylor & Francis.

Harvey, David. 2008. "The right to the city." *The City Reader* 6: 23–40.

— 2012. *Rebel Cities: From the Right to the City to the Urban Revolution*. London, UK: Verso Books.

Havel, Vaclav, and Paul Wilson. 1985. "The power of the powerless." *International Journal of Politics* 15, nos 3/4: 23–96.

Heiman, Michael. 1990, "From 'Not in My Backyard!' to 'Not in Anybody's Backyard!'"

Herbert, Steve. 2005. "The trapdoor of community." *Annals of the Association of American Geographers* 95, no. 4: 850–65.

Hirsch, Arnold, and Joseph Logsdon. 1992. *Creole New Orleans: Race and Americanization*. Baton Rouge, LA: LSU Press.

Hogue, Teresa. 1993. "Community-based collaboration: Community wellness multiplied." Paper delivered at Oregon State University, Oregon Center for Community Leadership.

Holman, Bob. 1987. "Research from the underside." *British Journal of Social Work* 17, no. 6: 669–83.

Horne, Jed. 2008. *Breach of Faith: Hurricane Katrina and the Near Death of a Great American City*. New York, NY: Random House Trade Paperbacks.

Hummel, Rebecca, and Douglas Ahlers. 2007. *Lessons from Katrina: How a Community Can Spearhead Successful Disaster Recovery*. Broadmoor Project, Belfer Center for Science and International Affairs, John F. Kennedy School of Government, Harvard University.

Hunter, Floyd. 1969. *Community Power Structure: A Study of Decision Makers*. Chapel Hill, NC: University of North Carolina Press.

Ishiwata, Eric. 2011. "We are seeing people we didn't know exist: Katrina and the neoliberal erasure of race." In *The Neoliberal Deluge: Hurricane Katrina, Late Capitalism, and the Remaking of New Orleans*, edited by Cedric Johnson, 32–59. Minneapolis, MN: University of Minnesota Press.

Jacobs, Jane. 1961. *The Death and Life of Great American Cities*. New York, NY: Vintage.

Jargowsky, Paul. 1997. *Poverty and Place: Ghettos, Barrios, and the American City*. New York, NY: Russell Sage Foundation.

Johnson, Cedric. 2011a. "Charming accommodations: Progressive urbanism meets privatization in Brad Pitt's make it right foundation." In *The Neoliberal Deluge: Hurricane Katrina, Late Capitalism, and the Remaking of New Orleans*, edited by Cedric Johnson, 187–224. Minneapolis, MN: University of Minnesota Press.

— 2011b. "Introduction: The neoliberal deluge." In *The Neoliberal Deluge: Hurricane Katrina, Neoliberalism, and the Remaking of New Orleans*, edited by Cedric Johnson, xvii–xlix. Minneapolis, MN: University of Minnesota Press.

Kaldor, Mary, and Sabine Selchow. 2013. "The 'bubbling up' of subterranean politics in Europe." *Journal of civil society* 9, no. 1: 78–99.

Kates, Robert William, Craig Colten, Shirley Laska, and Stephen Leatherman. 2006. "Reconstruction of New Orleans after Hurricane Katrina: A research perspective." *Proceedings of the National Academy of Sciences* 103, no. 40: 14653–60.

Katz, Daniel, and Robert Kahn. 1966. *The Social Psychology of Organizations*. Chichester, NY: Wiley Press.

Katz, Richard, and Peter Mair. 1995. "Changing models of party organization and party democracy." *Party Politics* 1, no. 1: 5–28.

King, Gary, Robert Keohane, and SidneyVerba. 1994. *Designing Social Inquiry: Scientific Inference in Qualitative Research*. Princeton, NJ: Princeton University Press.

Klein, Naomi. 2007. *The Shock Doctrine: The Rise of Disaster Capitalism*. New York, NY: Metropolitan Books.

Klijn, Eric-Hans, and Chris Skelcher. 2007. "Democracy and governance networks: Compatible or not?" *Public Administration* 85, no. 3: 587–608.

Knoke, David. 1988. "Incentives in collective action organizations." *American Sociological Review* 53, no. 3: 311–29.

Konrad, Ellen. 1996. "A multidimensional framework for conceptualizing human services integration initiatives." *New Directions for Evaluation* 69: 5–19.

Kooiman, Jan. 1993. *Modern Governance: New Government-Society Interactions*. Thousand Oaks, CA: Sage Publications.

Ladson-Billings, Gloria, and William Tate. 1995. "Toward a critical race theory of education." *Teachers College Record* 97, no. 1: 47.

Lake, Robert. 2017. "Locating the social in social justice." *Annals of the American Association of Geographers*, 1–9.

Latour, Bruno. 2005. *Reassembling the Social: An Introduction to Actor-Network-Theory*. Oxford, UK: Oxford University Press.

Lawson, H. 2002. "Improving conceptual clarity, accuracy, and precision and facilitating more coherent institutional designs." In *The Contribution of Interprofessional Collaboration and Comprehensive Services to Teaching and Learning, The National Society for the Study of Education Yearbook*, 30–45.

Layton, Lyndsey. 2014. "In New Orleans, major school district closes traditional public schools for good." *Washington Post*, May 28.

Lefebvre, Henry. 1943. "The right to the city." In *Writings on Cities by Henry Lefebvre*, 63–181.

Leontidou, Lila. 2010. "Urban social movements in 'weak' civil societies: The right to the city and cosmopolitan activism in southern Europe." *Urban Studies* 47, no. 6: 1179–203.

Leutz, Walter. 1999. "Five laws for integrating medical and social services: Lessons from the United States and the United Kingdom." *Milbank Quarterly* 77, no. 1: 77–110.

Litterer, Joseph. 1973. *The Analysis of Organizations*. Chichester, NY: Wiley Press.

Logan, John R. 2006. "The impact of Katrina: Race and class in storm-damaged neighborhoods." Report by the Spatial Structures in the Social Science at Brown University. Accessed March 28, 2006: http://www.s4.brown.edu/katrina/report.pdf

Logan, John, and Gordana Rabrenovic. 1990. "Neighborhood associations: Their issues, their allies, and their opponents." *Urban Affairs Review* 26, no. 1: 68–94.

Lotta Continua. 1972. "Nehmen wir uns die Stadt: Klassenanalyse, Organisationspapier, Kampfprogramm: Beiträge der Lotta Continua zur Totalisierung der Kämpfe." *Trikont*, no. 29. As in Mayer 2009.

Lovell, Anne. 2011. "Who cares about care? Health care rationalization and the demise of a public hospital after Katrina." *Metro Politiques*. Accessed January 3, 2018: http://www.metropolitiques.eu/Who-cares-about-care-Health-care.html

Lowndes, Vivien, and Helen Sullivan. 2008. "How low can you go? Rationales and challenges for neighbourhood governance." *Public Administration – London* 86, no. 1: 53.

Lubet, Steven. 2015. "Ethics on the run." *New Rambler Review*, May: 15–34.

Lukes, Steven. 1974. *Power: A Radical View*. London, UK: Macmillan Press.

McNulty, Ian. 2012. "Meet the Mississippi: Exploring the New Orleans riverfront." *FrenchQuarter.com*. Accessed February 3, 2018: http://www.frenchquarter.com/sightseeing/riverfront.php

Marcuse, Peter. 2009. "From critical urban theory to the right to the city." *City* 13, nos 2–3: 185–97.

Mayer, Margit. 2009. "The 'Right to the City' in the context of shifting mottos of urban social movements." *City* 13, nos 2–3: 362–74.

Mayhew, David. 2002. *America's Congress: Actions in the Public Sphere, James Madison through Newt Gingrich*. New Haven, CT: Yale University Press.

Miles, Matthew, and Michael Huberman. 1994. *Qualitative Data Analysis: An Expanded Sourcebook*. London, UK: Sage Publications.

Miller, David. 1999. *Principles of Social Justice*. Boston, MA: Harvard University Press.

Mitchell, Don. 2003. *The Right to the City: Social Justice and the Fight for Public Space*. New York, NY: Guilford Press.

Mulford, Charles, and David Rogers. 1982. "Definitions and models." In *Interorganizational Coordination: Theory, Research and Implementation*, edited by David Whetten, 9–31.

Nagin, Ray. 2011. *Katrina's Secrets: Storms after the Storm*. Charleston, SC: CreateSpace Independent Publishing.

Nylen, William. 2003. "Participatory democracy versus elitist democracy. Lessons from Brazil." Houndmills and New York: Palgrave Macmillan.

Olds, Kris. 1998. "Urban mega-events, evictions and housing rights: The Canadian case." *Current Issues in Tourism* 1, no. 1: 2–46.

Perin, Constance. 1977. *Everything in Its Place: Social Order and Land Use in America*. Princeton University Press.

Peters, B. Guy, Jon Pierre, and Desmond King. 2005. "The politics of path dependency: Political conflict in historical institutionalism." *Journal of Politics* 67, no. 4: 1275–300.

Piven, Frances Fox, and Richard Cloward. 1979. *Poor People's Movements: Why They Succeed, How They Fail*. Vintage.

Polletta, Francesca. 2002. *Freedom Is an Endless Meeting: Democracy in American Social Movements*. Chicago, IL: University of Chicago Press.

Provan, Keith, and Patrick Kenis. 2008. "Modes of network governance: Structure, management, and effectiveness." *Journal of Public Administration Research and Theory* 18, no. 2: 229–52.

Purcell, Mark. 2002. "Excavating Lefebvre: The right to the city and its urban politics of the inhabitant." *GeoJournal* 58, nos 2–3: 99–108.

– 2006. "Urban democracy and the local trap." *Urban Studies* 43, no. 11: 1921–41.

– 2008. *Recapturing Democracy: Neoliberalization and the Struggle for Alternative Urban Futures*. New York, NY: Routledge.

Rabe, Barry. 1994. *Beyond NIMBY: Hazardous Waste Siting in Canada and the United States*. Cambridge, UK: Cambridge University Press.

Ramos, Dante. 2016. "To avoid housing nightmare, say 'yes in my back yard.'" *Boston Globe*, July 24, 2016.

Rawls, John. 1965. "Review of Richard B. Brandt, ed. Social Justice." *The Philosophical Review* 74, no. 3: 406–9.

References

– 2001. *Justice as Fairness: A Restatement.* Boston, MA: Harvard University Press.

Rhonheimer, Martin. 2015. "The true meaning of 'social justice': A catholic view of Hayek." *Economic Affairs* 35, no. 1: 35–51.

Rich, Richard. 2008. "The roles of neighborhood organizations in urban service delivery." *Journal of Urban Affairs* 1, no. 1: 81–93.

Rittenhouse, Diane, Laura Schmidt, Kevin Wu, and James Wiley. 2012. "The post-Katrina conversion of clinics in New Orleans to medical homes shows change is possible, but hard to sustain." *Health Affairs* 31, no. 8: 1729–38.

Rogers, Everett, James Dearing, and Dorine Bregman. 1988. "The anatomy of agenda-setting research." *Journal of Communication* 43, no. 2: 68–84.

Rogers, Richard A. 2006. "From cultural exchange to transculturation: A review and reconceptualization of cultural appropriation." *Communication Theory* 16, no. 4: 474–503.

Routledge, Paul, and Andrew Cumbers. 2013. *Global Justice Networks: Geographies of Transnational Solidarity.* Oxford University Press.

Rozell, Mark, and Clyde Wilcox. 1995. *God at the Grass Roots: The Christian Right in the 1994 Elections.* New York, NY: Rowman & Littlefield.

Scott, James. 1985. *Weapons of the Weak Everyday Forms of Peasant Resistance.* New Haven, CT: Yale University Press.

Selznick, Philip. 1949. *TVA and the Grass Roots: A Study of Politics and Organization.* Oakland, CA: University of California Press.

Smith, Teresa. 1999. "Neighbourhood and preventive strategies with children and families: What works?" *Children & Society* 13, no. 4: 265–77.

Sobel, Russell, and Peter Leeson. 2006. "Government's response to Hurricane Katrina: A public choice analysis." *Public Choice* 127, no. 1: 55–73.

Sørensen, Eva, and Jacob Torfing. 2005. "The democratic anchorage of governance networks." *Scandinavian Political Studies* 28, no. 3: 195.

Stablein, Ralph. 1996. "Data organization studies." In *Handbook for Organizational Studies,* edited by Stewart Clegg, Cynthia Hardy, and Walter Nord, 509–25. Thousand Oaks, CA: Sage Publications.

Stoker, Gerry. 1998. "Governance as theory: Five propositions." *International Social Science Journal* 50, no. 155: 17–28.

Surowiecki, James. 2005. *The Wisdom of Crowds.* London, UK: Abacus.

Swanstrom, Todd. 1985. *The Crisis of Growth Politics: Cleveland, Kucinich, and the Challenge of Urban Populism.* Philadelphia, PA: Temple University Press.

Szirom, Tricia, Jim Hyde, Zara Lasater, and Cathi Moore. 2002. "Working together – Integrated governance." Report prepared with Success Works Pty Ltd and the Centre for Health Outcomes and Innovations Research for the IPAA National Research Project 2000.

Tiebout, Charles. 1956. "A pure theory of local expenditures." *Journal of Political Economy* 64, no. 5: 416–24.

Tierney, Kathleen, Christine Bevc, and Erica Kuligowski. 2006. "Metaphors matter: Disaster myths, media frames, and their consequences in Hurricane Katrina." *Annals of the American Academy of Political and Social Science* 604, no. 1: 57–81.

United Nations Center for Human Settlements. 2001. "Policy dialogue series: Number 1 women and urban governance." New York: UNCHS (Habitat). As in Purcell 2002.

Vickers, Geoffrey. 1972. *Freedom in a Rocking Boat.* London, UK: Penguin Books.

Walker, Donna, Margaretha Geertsema, and Barbara Barnett. 2009. "Inverting the inverted pyramid: A conversation about the use of feminist theories to teach journalism." *Feminist Teacher* 19, no. 3: 177–8.

Walker, Robert, Gill Dix, and Meg Huby. 1992. *Working the Social Fund.* Blue Ridge Summit, PA: Bernan Press.

Wilson, James Q., and George Kelling. 1982. "The police and neighborhood safety: Broken windows." *Atlantic Monthly* 127: 29–38.

Winer, Michael, and Karen Ray. 1994. *Collaboration Handbook: Creating, Sustaining, and Enjoying the Journey.* St Paul, MN: Amherst H. Wilder Foundation.

Worldwide Conference on the Right to Cities Free from Discrimination and Inequality. 2002. Conference in Porto Alegre, Brazil. As in Purcell 2002.

Young, Iris Marion. 1990. "Activist challenges to deliberative democracy." *Political Theory* 29, no. 5: 670–90.

Zimbardo, Phillip. 1969. "The human choice: Individuation, reason, and order versus deindividuation, impulse, and chaos." *Nebraska Symposium on Motivation.* Lincoln, NE: University of Nebraska Press.

Index